FLIGHT TO TRANSFORMATION

Peace, Love, Abundance

LARRY SMITH

Copyright © 2017 by Larry Smith

Flight to Transformation

Published by BurmanBooks Media Corp.
260 Queens Quay West, Suite 1102
Toronto, Ontario
Canada M5J 2N3

All rights reserved. No part of this publication may be reproduced, stored in a retrieval system, or transmitted in any form by any process—electronic, photocopying, recording, or otherwise—without the prior written consent of BurmanBooks Media Corp.

Editor: Effie Sotiropoulos
Cover & Interior Design: Clarissa D'Costa

Distribution:
NewLeaf Distribution
401 Thorton Rd.
Lithia Springs, GA 30122-1557

ISBN: 978-1988757001

Printed and bound in Canada

This is a two-part book: The Flight, and The Transformation.

The Flight is a brief memoir of the life of Captain Larry Smith. It exposes the details of how alcohol, cocaine and self-will turned his incredible life into a living hell.

The Transformation features author Captain Smith's profound insight into humanity and spirituality as he examines the differences between perception and reality, pleasure and happiness, ego and spirit, and time and eternity.

"Acceptance that we are spiritual beings having a human experience is the basis to sustaining a spiritual awakening." -Larry Smith

CONTENTS

Forward *(The Flight)*	**7**
Introduction - The Four Levels of Transformation *(The Transformation)*	**43**
Taking the First Step – The Transformation Begins Here and Now	**55**
Hope – The Bridge Between Surrender and Faith	**63**
The Conscious Decision to Have Faith	**73**
Getting Real by Facing Reality	**83**
Rising Above Ego-Driven Shame	**93**

FLIGHT TO TRANSFORMATION

Entirely Ready for Change	**101**
Empowerment Through Vulnerability	**113**
The Joy of Atonement, Reparations and Forgiveness	**123**
Merging with the Mind of God – Just for Today	**139**
Make Me a Channel of Thy Peace	**149**
Recognition of Transformation	**159**
A Step-by-Step Spiritual Summary	**170**
References	**180**

The Flight

Childhood

Illusions of grandeur, a dash of fear, and a persistent Napoleonic complex best describe my youth. Right from the start I was different. I felt more, I worried more, and I strived obsessively to be liked. I constantly daydreamed about being an athlete, a leader, or a politician. In any situation, I sought to be in the limelight. I never passed up the opportunity to jump in a photo or catch a glimpse of myself in a mirror.

As far back as I can remember, I was a sensitive youngster who internally felt other people's pain. I hated bullies, and at times I risked certain death by sticking up for the underdog in a fight.

I set my visions on marrying my second-grade teacher. I knew that she loved me as much as I loved her. Miss Gerding was exquisitely gorgeous. She had thick, wavy, brunette hair down to her shoulders that she would occasionally wear up in a bun, exposing her white, silky neck. She possessed soft, sparkly green-gray eyes and a perfect figure. I didn't know anything about sex, but she stimulated my developing brain to release chemicals that had never been released before, and weren't released again until puberty.

I would stay after school every day and clean the blackboards; she would reward me by driving me home in her 1946 pea-green Plymouth. She would literally lean into me so I could kiss her cheek goodbye – the 1950's were obviously different times. I looked forward to that kiss every day. I was shattered at the end of the school year when she told me she was moving to Tennessee and would not be teaching at my school any longer.

For the next year, I would sit in Sunday Mass and daydream about Miss Gerding returning. I tuned out my surroundings and visualized her entrance through the back doors of the church, strewn atop a gold gurney being carried by shirtless Egyptian slaves. She would be draped in a lacy white wedding dress, and as they carried her down the aisle she would point to the front of the church and gesture for me to meet her at the altar. The marriage ceremony was usually interrupted with my mother poking me in the ribs and telling me to pay attention to the priest.

I still wonder what became of Miss Gerding. Did she continue to teach? Did she marry and have children? If alive, my fantasy childhood bride would be in her 80s today and I am certain she would still be as beautiful and intriguing as she was in 1957 when I kissed her cheek one last time.

My childhood need for attention was fulfilled by my self-cultivated spirited sense of humor. This trait, and hyperactivity (now known as ADHD) made me a challenging student for every teacher unlucky enough to have me in their class. My grades were average and every report card contained the commented, "Capable of doing much better."

The Beginning...

I was born on November 27, 1950, in an Ohio town ironically named Defiance. No other birthplace name could have been more fitting for my personality; defiance of the rules and a gut-wrenching persistence to achieve whatever I set my sights on would later explain both my successes and my failures.

Small Town, USA

I spent the first 17 years of my life in my hometown, Deshler, Ohio. Deshler was a close-knit community that predominantly consisted of farming families. Most folks were of German descent. This partially explains why most events, from church socials to polka dances, featured a frothy, golden potently intoxicating brew; every occasion, or lack of occasion, was an excuse for a cold beer. Although the census of Deshler was around 1800 people, the population supported five full-service bars. We also had an abundance of Christian churches that brought a nice balance to the over-indulging that often took place in the community.

Deshler, which was at the crossroads of the B&O Railroad, had the nickname "The Corn City" and was known for growing hybrid seed corn. It is the North-South, East-West crossroad of the Baltimore and Ohio Railroad. The

B&O is one of only four railroads on the Monopoly board.

I attended kindergarten through senior high school in the same building. I was blessed with three sisters and a traditional Midwest upbringing. My parents were extremely hard-working people. Outside of work, the focus was on our entire family, which included immediate and extended family members. To my knowledge, every adult and most of the teens in the family drank beer.

I loved sports and wanted desperately to be an athlete. Disregarding my lack of strength, coordination and other obvious shortcomings, I made the freshman basketball team. As a freshman, I stood at 5 feet 2 inches and made the team only because too few boys tried out.

The team consisted of only seven players and a six foot nine coach who had just graduated from Findlay College. The standing joke was that if two guys fouled out, Coach Shockey would play with four players rather than risk his reputation by putting me in the game. Six games passed and I still hadn't set so much as a foot on the court. Much to my embarrassment, by the fourth quarter, the cheerleaders began rallying for my presence on the court by chanting, "We want Smitty! We want Smitty!"

Coach Shockey finally broke down and put me in a game that were up in by 25 points with a couple of minutes left on the clock. Quickly, I lived up to his expectations of my inabilities as I hurtled my first official shot two feet over the top of the backboard. I still remember the look on the referee's face as he blew the whistle, shook his head, and smiled at me all in the same moment. I don't recall the cheerleaders chanting my name after that.

As funny as it was, it still hurt and added to my mindset that I would never be good enough. Albeit unintentionally, my father added to this insecure belief that I didn't measure up. Depression-era dads tended to use shame-based parenting techniques to motivate their underperforming children.

Dad would leave for work early in the morning six days a week. He would return home at 5:40 p.m. week days and 12:30 p.m. on Saturdays. I would try to chum around with dear old Dad in the evenings and Saturday afternoon by assisting him in his woodworking shop. There was one major problem with my attempts to get closer to my father - I would start bleeding at the sight of a power tool. This, in addition to my total lack of woodworking aptitude, left me with only one purpose in those bonding moments: broom sweeper. I excelled at that function, but I realized early on that it would be an unenjoyable full time endeavor.

From feedback, I received from my teachers, my parents and the Catholic Church, I had accepted that I was not a good boy. Subsequently, I learned to associate fun and pleasure with guilt and shame. I started sipping beer at a very young age while sitting on my dad's lap. I would sprinkle salt on the foam to minimize the bitter taste. I now know that both salt and alcohol release the brain chemical dopamine, the neurotransmitter in the brain responsible for delivering pleasure.

My only sex education came from my older friend, Harley, who had learned it first-hand from Janice, the nine-year-old girl down the street.
Janice once cornered me alone in Harley's garage and directed me to feel her breasts. As I started down inside her T-shirt, she smacked me and said, "Go up from the bottom, dummy." Instead, I ran from the garage. Not sure if my intent to feel Janice's breast was a sin, I anguished over reporting it in my next confession. I justified my actions by thinking that, since I didn't contact Janice's nipple, I did not commit a sin.

As I grew into my teens, I was never denied beer if I drank it at home. This practice lasted until I was 15 when I started riding in cars with my buddies. In small-town USA, it was barely a challenge to buy alcohol as a minor. With a case of beer in tow, my friends and I would roam the back streets of Deshler and vast cornfields that surrounded the town drinking and throwing empties at stop signs. Obviously, several cases of beer, muscle cars and bored teenagers created havoc and danger to those involved. One event I can still visualize today involved racing down Main Street in the back of a pick-up truck with three guys and a keg. The drive accelerated and threw "Big Bill" over the back onto the pavement. Bill's foot got caught on the bumper and he was dragged on his back for 50 feet before he came loose. We were so drunk we poured beer on his back and continued the ride. These activities brought angst to the community; nevertheless, many of the folks in Deshler viewed this behavior as a rite of passage.

I got my first job at the ripe age of 12 when I began working at my dad's gas station, Smith Auto Service, under the supervision of my uncle Bob. Dad and Uncle Bob had extremely strong work ethics. I made a whopping 50 cents an hour. I shuddered as Uncle Bob would point his finger at me and say, "If I'm paying you 50 cents an hour, you had better be working every minute of that hour!" – and he was serious.

By the time I was 16, I was drinking every weekend. Looking back, I never actually liked the taste of alcohol, but I loved the effect. Alcohol numbed my fears and quieted the voices that told me I didn't measure up. Deep-seated feelings of unworthiness hounded me through my early years, and those same feelings amplified as I entered the adult world.

I covered up my insecurities with arrogant and boisterous behavior, and I was a master at finding faults in others. My humor often overstepped the bounds of common decency; I was full of false pride. I counted on alcohol, and later drugs, to make me feel whole.

I played rhythm guitar in the local garage band. This was a temporary ego boost because all the band members were older and cool. Ted Lee, the band's leader, sold me my first guitar for $35, and the price included a few lessons. Surprised at how quickly I learned to play complicated chords, Ted asked me to join his band, The Shadesmen.

My lack of maturity appeared one Friday night during a gig at the McComb Legion Hall. I attempted to mimic Peter Frampton on stage and slammed my guitar into my amplifier. Ted politely suggested that I was not quite ready for prime time.

I graduated high school on May 27, 1968 at exactly $17\frac{1}{2}$ years old. A week later, my graduating class traveled by train to Washington, D.C. On the train ride home, we learned that Bobby Kennedy had been shot and killed. The sixties were a strange time to come of age. The JFK, MLK and RFK assassinations, a new era of rock 'n' roll, and the protest movements left me with uncanny feelings of discontentment.

Young men from my hometown, only a few years older than me, were coming home in body bags. These young, small-town farm boys had left with a sense of innocent patriotism only to be thrown into a mindless war contrived for political and corporate gain. We witnessed a lack of training and military leadership while occupying a war zone where heroin, pot and booze added to the mayhem, fear, and devastation.

This chaotic world filled me with one basic emotion: fear. I was a cocky teenager who drank and acted out because I was afraid to face the future. I should have been more concerned about my reckless self-sabotaging behaviors, such as, fighting, drinking, and driving cars at obscene rates of speed.

Since I wasn't college-bound, I knew military service was inevitable. I was ready to enlist in the Navy, as my father had 26 years before. Dad went on to fight in World War II from the deck of the USS Enterprise. I had signed the paperwork to enlist, but I had not yet sent it into The Department of the Navy when my life took a horrendous turn.

While filling in as a pump jockey one evening at Uncle Bob's gas station, a young man named Dennis Meyer pulled in wearing an Air Force uniform. Dennis informed me that he had joined the Toledo Air National Guard. The 180th TFG was located just 32 miles north of Deshler, yet I had never heard of it. Dennis bragged about the benefits of being in the Air Guard as opposed to my plan of enlisting in the Navy. I followed his suggestion and made an appointment with the Air Guard's recruiter, Senior Master Sergeant Jerry Baum.

Life is full of decisions. The decision to work that evening at the gas station was a seemingly small choice; however, that one decision totally changed my life. That young airman, whom I barely knew, played a profound role in the direction I would take. Sadly, 18 months later, he drowned in the Maumee River halfway between the Guard Base and Deshler. He had averted being shot at in Vietnam only to die a tragic death at 20 years old because of a decision he made to go fishing.

The Military

On August 23, 1968, at the ripe old age of 17, I enlisted in the Air National Guard. I was so naïve about what I was doing that when I took the enlistment oath, I swore into the International Guard, not the Air National Guard. My swearing-in officer and new boss, Captain Jim Kaifas, laughed out loud at my ignorance since I didn't even know the name of the military service to which I had just made a six-year commitment.

In September 1968, I boarded a C-47, which is the same as a DC 3, except with nets for seats. We took off from the Toledo Express Airport at sunset and headed for Lackland Air Force Base in San Antonio, Texas. We stopped to pick up more new recruits and stayed overnight at Lockbourne AFB (now Rickenbacker) in Columbus, Ohio. I didn't sleep well that evening for two reasons: one was the memory of the look of utter sadness on my parents' faces as I boarded the WWII prop plane in Toledo; the other was the loud noise of C-130s doing engine run-ups on the nearby flight line. At the time, I had no idea that 25 years later I would have logged 2500 flight hours in that noisy C-130 Hercules.

My first military ID card stated that I stood 5'5" and weighed 112 pounds. Years later, that very ID card would get me into a heap of trouble. To go with my lack of size and strength, I shaved only once a week whether I needed it or not. In uniform, people confused me with being a boy scout.

The Vietnam War gained momentum and we had already lost several young men from Deshler. When asked by the recruiter what field I preferred to go into, I thought, *do something safe for a change and say you want a desk job* – so I did. I was assigned to a Combat Support Squadron in the Accounting and Finance Office at Toledo Express Airport. Immediately after my release from Active Duty, I took a full-time Civil Service job working in the Comptroller office at the Air National Guard base.

My job included preparing the payroll for the base personnel and, thus, I knew almost everyone by name. I enjoyed helping the troops with their payroll concerns. Most of all, I loved working with the 25 fighter pilots of the 112 Tactical

Fighter Squadron. The mystique of flying super-sonic, single-seat fighters created a burning desire in me to be one of them.

In the military, my drinking escalated. Stopping by the club for a few beers after work was condoned as a means of fostering morale. My morale always needed a boost, so I was a regular at the combined NCO and Officers Club on the base.

I was a fast burner in the enlisted ranks and I made Technical Sergeant E-6 in four years. That was the only thing on my side when I started to pursue a career as an Air Force Fighter Pilot. My lack of a college education and the fact that I failed the pilot training qualifying exam greatly diminished my chances of being chosen for Officer Candidate School and USAF Pilot Training.

Still, I cut out a picture of the T-38 jet trainer just as it was lifting off the runway and kept it under the glass on my accounting desk. I visualized myself as the pilot in the picture, screaming down the runway, pulling back on the stick, and lifting that sleek white jet into the air. I realized then that visualization without action is hallucination.

I started taking night classes at the University of Toledo to earn college credits in my seemingly hopeless pursuit to become a pilot. My first college professor, Dr. Adams, informed me that I was not college material and I should consider taking up a trade. He stated that he had never failed a student but I was close to being his first. It was May, 1970, the same quarter as the Kent State shootings. Due to all the campus unrest, all Mid-Am colleges decided to simply give pass-or-fail grades for that quarter. This administrative decision was the only reason I didn't begin my college career with a D or an F. The Kent State massacre salvaged my grade point average right before the summer break.

I ignored Dr. Adams' discouraging remarks and pressed on the following fall in pursuit of a higher education. I received A's in my next two classes and enjoyed a 4.0 average after 12 credit hours. After four years of night classes, I completed two years of college with an amazing 3.7 GPA.

Despite working full-time, being in the Air Guard and attending night school, I still found time to drink. I was prudent about finances, except for the high cost of drinking and drag racing. I saved money out of every check and made two large capital purchases: one was a new bright orange 1969 Plymouth Roadrunner, and the other, a mobile home. My friend John Budde from high school, who was also in the Air Guard, moved in to share the expenses of trailer park living in Swanton, Ohio. From Swanton, it was a reasonable commute to the Guard Base and to the University of Toledo.

In one of my early psychology classes, I learned about Maslow's hierarchy of needs. I studied it objectively and then declared that I had reached the pinnacle of the theory known as Self-Actualization. Yes, at the age of 21, I felt I had advanced to the highest levels of mental, intellectual, and emotional maturity. Rarely had such a feat been met at such a young age, and I told myself I most certainly could not have arrived at this level without the help of booze and pot. Certainly, this form of arrogance was to cover-up those underlying feelings of low self-esteem.

During this time, I stopped going to Mass and only prayed when deemed it necessary. I was dating my high school sweetheart, but I had a real problem with fidelity. In fact, I was a serial cheater. We attract what we are, and I attracted other narcissist cheaters who possessed the same character defects as myself: grandiosity, dishonesty, and extreme self-centeredness.

Vision Comes True

The year was 1974, and my Air Guard unit had one pilot training slot allotted for that year. There were six potential pilot candidates: two touting master's degrees, three with bachelor's degrees, and me, with two years of college. We had all passed the written exams (for me, it took two attempts) and the stringent Air Force pilot physical exam. The six candidates waited with bated breath for Colonel Charlie Bell to decide which one of us fine young men would attend pilot training that year.

One evening, while drunk and rolling on the floor of The Club NCO-Officers Club with my good friend, Jeff Davoll, Colonel Bell approached me. He pulled me up by my hair, and said, "Smitty, anybody that gets as drunk as you will make a damned good fighter pilot. I am sending you." The vision of pulling that T-38 off the runway just got a lot closer to becoming a reality, but first I had to complete Officer Training School in Knoxville, Tennessee, and Flight Screening School in Hondo, Texas.

Air Force Pilot Training

In October of 1974, I arrived at Undergraduate Air Force Pilot Training (UPT) at Williams Air Force Base in Chandler, Arizona. The pilot instructors and other student pilots could not figure out how a guy with only two years of college even got there. In fact, because I wasn't a college graduate, Colonel Bell had to obtain a special wavier from the Pentagon to send me to pilot training. He must not have mentioned the other candidates in his request.

Air Force pilot training was a blast. The long hours of studying paid off with the thrill of strapping into a super-sonic jet and doing things in the air I could never have imagined. Acrobatic maneuvers, fingertip formations or buzzing just above the treetops at 500 mph were everyday activities. I loved the thrill of being in control of these incredible flying machines – it was the best rush ever.

Despite my dedication to flying, my drinking landed me in trouble several times that year – once, after dumping my motorcycle while running from the Air Police, and another time for pulling strippers off the stage in the Officers Club. Today, either of these offenses would bring an instant court martial. Ignoring the threats from my commander, I pressed on partying like a madman.

The Air Force had an over-abundance of pilots because the end of the Vietnam War was near. Thus, the standards to graduate were higher than normal. More than half of the student pilots in my class washed out of training. At the end of training, my Flight Commander called me into his office for a meeting. He told me he believed I could make it through pilot training, but I was not good enough to fly fighters. He understood that my Air National Guard unit only had fighters, so he suggested I find another unit with transport aircraft that would take me.

I was humiliated. I promised him I would be much better in the next phase of training. I boldly pronounced, "I have to fly fighters. Period." He said, "We'll see," and arranged for me to have an outstanding T-38 Instructor Pilot.
As it turned out, I was assigned to the best, yet most demanding instructor on the base. Lieutenant Don Teeples was a short, skinny redhead from Oklahoma, and his reputation for setting extremely high standards struck fear in the hearts of student pilots. I was no exception.

April 28, 1975, was the day of my first flight in the T-38 Talon, the jet I had a picture of under the glass of my desk for five years. I was excited and scared, yet confident. As we approached the aircraft, tail number 62-3667, Lieutenant Don preached to me that the takeoff in a T-38 happens so quickly that most students don't get the gear up on time and, consequently, over-speed the gear doors. He threatened, "Smith, if you don't get the gear up on time, I'll break your f-ing arm!"

I had never been so motivated to do something perfectly in my life. So much so that on takeoff roll, after I pushed up the throttles and lit the afterburner, I immediately put my left hand on the gear handle. Flashes of the picture on my desk appeared as we began the take roll. Soon we were going so fast that it seemed the runway was closing in around me. The instant I pulled the stick back to lift off with my right hand, I immediately raised the gear with my left hand. The moment I had been envisioning for years had arrived: we were three feet off the runway, going 200 miles per hour with the gear up. I was breathing so hard that I was on the brink of hyperventilating. With pressured breath, I uttered the required radio call, "Albuquerque Center, AWOL 42 climbing through 10,000 feet for flight level two-four -zero."

Then, I heard Lt. Teeples, from the back seat of the jet, shout, "Hot-damn! You're no weak dick. You'll be fine." Later in the flight, we performed aerobatics and broke sound barrier by going supersonic - over 1.0 Mach.
My confidence was genuine and no longer driven by blind arrogance. I knew then that nothing could stop me from getting my silver wings, and becoming an Air Force fighter pilot.

I immediately began to appreciate his having instilled in me the need to strive for absolute perfection in aviation. My aviation skills increased and my genuine confidence level rose to the point of obnoxiousness. He later gave me an outstanding evaluation and I was designated fighter qualified, graduating near the top of my class.

During pilot training, my girlfriend in Ohio threatened to leave me if I didn't marry her, so I went home on Christmas break and got married. I immediately started having trouble with the vows part of the arrangement and single-handedly proceeded to destroy the trust that my new wife, Vickie, had in me. I spent the little time I had off from studying and flying drinking beer and flying model airplanes with my buddies. One of my best friends, Don Wolfe, had mastered flying model airplanes. Wolfman, as I called him, was six months ahead of me in training and was the other Toledo Air Guard pilot at Williams AFB. Don was a native of Coshocton, Ohio, and had a reputation of being a fighter pilot's fighter pilot, and the best student pilot to attend pilot training in the history of Williams AFB. Don would remain in my life for the next 40 years.

In the year and a half that I was away for training, the Toledo Air National Guard experienced three major F-100 crashes. Captain Tommy Truehaft, while rolling into a target at the gunnery range, experienced a hydraulic failure and had to punch out of the jet. Of course, the aircraft exploded on impact, and the force from the rocket-expulsion type ejection seat left Tommy with severe back injuries. The compression on his vertebrae left him 1½ inches shorter. A year later, he returned to flying.

The second crash involved my friend Lt. Mike Mann. Mike and I had similar features and many people in the unit confused us with each other. He and another pilot decided to put on an unauthorized airshow over a lake in northern Michigan. While flying fast, low and inverted, Mike lost control and made the decision to eject. In talking with the men who retrieved him, they reported that Mike went into trees at 450 mph still in the ejection seat.

The last accident happened late on a Friday afternoon in May of 1975. My mentor, friend and Commander, Col. Charles Bell, died in a crash landing on

Runway 7 at Toledo Express Airport.

My friend Don Wolfe came to my home early on Saturday morning to deliver the news that Col. Bell, the man who had opened the door to my aviation career, was gone. With my Toledo unit having two deaths and three crashes while I was in pilot training, I woke up to the danger involved in flying single engine, single-seat fighters. Every mission must be planned and completed with focus and discipline. The words of an old General would ring in my ears before every flight: "Integrity is doing the right thing even when no one is watching."

Despite drinking problems, bar fights and black eyes, on October 18, 1975, I received my coveted Silver Air Force Pilot Wings.

As I left Williams AFB, my classmates signed my yearbook with grim predictions of my demise. Only a few pilots in the class were assigned to flying fighters. The aging F-100 was known as the "Widow Maker." My classmates proclaimed that my chances of experiencing a long lifespan were nil. They signed off my book with quotes like, "It was nice knowing ya!"

Survival Training

Next, I attended Water Survival Training in Florida, followed by Ground Survival and POW Training in Washington State. Survival schools were challenging and grueling. Water survival included being dragged behind a high-speed boat while trying to jettison my parachute, and parasailing into the Biscayne Bay and floating on a raft for hours in shark-infested waters.

Nothing could have prepared me for POW (Prisoner of War) training. Living in the cold, snowy mountains without food and shelter for a week was the best part. Being stripped, beaten up, and locked up in small boxes for long periods of time was not what I had visualized as part of my training. I was released from the mock POW camp and arrived back in Ohio on November 22, 1975, the day of my sister Luann's wedding. My dad was disgusted with the Air Force when he saw my battered and bruised body. I was exhausted. Still, I was not too tired to drink copious amount of beer at the reception.

After being humiliated in survival schools, I attended a seven-month transition course into the F-100 in Tucson, Arizona, to become a fighter pilot.

Fighter Pilot Training

The daily life of a fighter pilot was everything it was cracked up to be and more. Performing maneuvers such as air-to-air combat, dropping bombs, shooting rockets, low level strafing 100 rounds of 20 mm shells every two seconds, and conducting night air-to-air refueling was more challenging and accelerating than I could have ever imagined. I graduated from the F-100 course with the top academic record in my class, and was second in accuracy on the bombing and strafing of targets.

Hanging around the bar with fighter pilots gets more than a little crazy. Drinking games included Dead Bug; when the pilot who bought the last round, or a past POW, yelled, "Dead bug," the last person to hit the floor on his back with arms and legs flailing wildly above him (like a bug dying a tragic death) would have to buy the next round. This is quite expensive for the loser, so the competition to avoid being the last sucker standing was brutal.

I witnessed fighter pilots eating raw eggs, opening beer bottles with their teeth (not twist-offs) and, worst of all, a warrior who ate his beer glass to amuse his peers. I heard he later went on to become a General. Seeing other pilots behaving worse than myself gave me a warped sense of normality.

I arrived back at the Toledo Air Guard unit and became known as a "Guard Bum." This is the name for pilots that didn't have jobs outside of the Air Guard. I was flying to gain experience, and that's exactly what happened.

After learning to fly in sunny Arizona, the rain, snow, wind and fog in Northwest Ohio was alarming. The competition between pilots was fierce at times, and the demands of the senior aviators in the squadron were stringent. One time, as flying number four, a four-ship formation, right after takeoff, I had a wing slat hang-up. To keep the airplane level, I accidentally pulled the throttle out of afterburner. I lost altitude and pulled away from the formation and noticed

I was uncomfortably close to the treetops. I got the afterburner relit and rejoined the formation. Instead of questioning what happened, the flight leader proceeded to chew my ass out over the radio for not being in close enough formation. On the ground, he continued with his barrage of criticism and didn't care at all about my excuses.

No matter how badly the senior guys screwed up, the blame would always roll downhill to the new Lieutenants. Flying regularly in bad weather, being criticized often, and surviving multiple emergencies, I eventually became a damn good fighter pilot, as Col. Bell said I would be. I received an accelerated promotion to Captain because of the awards I achieved in training.

During this time as a Guard bum, I developed a new goal - becoming an Airline Pilot. This would require a degree.

Finishing College

In August of 1977, I finished my bachelor's degree and graduated cum laude with a BS in Business Management and a minor in Psychology. Not bad for a guy that had done so poorly on the SAT's that he was advised to go back and take high school classes in Reading and English before entering college.

Ironically, the last elective I took during my final quarter of college at the University of Toledo was a class called "Alcohol." When alcoholics were discussed in class, I knew I wasn't one of those people. I got an A in the class.

Now, my sights were firmly set on getting an airline job – so much so that I did not bother to attend my own college graduation, arrogantly looking at it as an insignificant event.

Babies & Braniff

With a bachelor's degree in hand, and closing in on 1000 hours of flying time, I started filling out commercial pilot applications. I then completed an expensive three-month Flight Engineer course at Dallas Love Field. The Veterans Administration paid for the schooling, and upon completion I was certified on the Boeing 727. In May of 1978, Braniff International Airlines hired me as a Second Officer. After a month based in Minneapolis, I was transferred to Kansas City.

I moved in to an upscale commuter-home in Gladstone, MO. I would occasionally have conjugal visits with my wife in Toledo, only seeing her when I would go back to fly for the Air Guard. I felt like was living a double life. While in KC MO, I was a wild and crazy bachelor; in Ohio, I was a married Air Guard pilot that spent more time at the base and in the bar than with my wife. The trips back to Ohio became less and less frequent.

On October 9, 1979, in Smithville Missouri, my first son, Nathan, was born. It was love at first sight. He was a bright light in my rapidly diminishing life. Still, the marriage continued to slide downhill.

In 1981, I abruptly and prematurely quit the Air National Guard, even though I had just spent two months learning to fly the A-7 Corsair. During my training in A-7 school, I found myself in serious trouble once again after a wild night of drinking at the Davis-Monthan Officers' Club. My bad behavior in the military wasn't funny anymore. The unit commander was getting tired of seeing my face in his office and he was relieved when I made the request to resign.

Later that year, on October 13, my second son, Lucas, was born. He had several health problems in his first tender year of life. He endured surgery on his esophagus at seven weeks old, and later that year he came down with near-fatal spinal meningitis. For the first time in years, I prayed. My brief reconnection with God ended once Lucas recovered from his illnesses. I loved my sons more than I had ever loved anyone or anything, but because of my selfish drinking, I was unable to display my feelings appropriately. I was living in a fog caused by a disease known as alcoholism - a disease that tells you that you don't have it. I could see it in other people, but not in myself.

Even in this state, it was important to me to be financially responsible when it came to my family, but I was not emotionally available as a father, or as a husband, simply because of my powerlessness over alcohol. Even as an alcoholic, I kept driving forward, constantly setting my sights on making money and working diligently at looking good. I was so skilled at putting on the act of being happy and successful that no one could see the pain and despair that was growing inside of me.

Real Estate and Downward Spiral

I had walked away from the military after 12 years not knowing that Braniff Airlines would soon file Chapter 7 bankruptcy. With the airline industry cutting back, and the fact that I have burned my bridges in the Toledo Air Guard, there was little hope of finding another flying job. Needing to feed two babies, I started down the road to a new career in real estate. I completed the classes and testing to become a licensed real estate agent and, later, a licensed broker.

My timing for getting into real estate appeared to be dismal. Mortgage rates were more than 16 percent and many realtors were running for the hills. Recognizing that people still needed to buy and sell homes, I saw an opportunity and seized it. I specialized in alternative types of financing such as land contracts, purchase money mortgages, lease options and lease purchases. Soon, I became the sales leader in my company, and my success drew attention from many of the real estate companies in Toledo. Several brokerages and builders started recruiting me. I was most impressed with a company that offered me an interesting package. It included a $1000-per-month salary (unheard of for commissioned real estate agents), an all-expenses-paid condominium, a membership to Brandywine Country Club and, best of all, an abundance of cocaine. I was back to living the high life – pun intended.

It didn't take long to figure out that the business model contrived by a fellow cokehead wasn't working out. In fact, the company had committed fraud and failed soon after. Fortunately, I hadn't been part of any of the fraudulent activities and my excellent real estate reputation stayed intact. I went to work for a prestigious real estate firm and became an instant success.

I had turned to buying, selling, and rehabbing foreclosures. I was a clever realtor and was respected as a hard-working salesman by other professionals in the Toledo area. I assembled groups of accountants, insurance brokers, stockbrokers, and investment advisors to invest in income-producing properties that were in foreclosure with the local banks and savings and loans (S&Ls). I was always the managing general partner in these investments, and I gave each project with the name BIRE (Belief in Real Estate) and a roman numeral. Some of the BIRE projects made money over time, and some of them made money upfront when the Savings and Loan companies would allow us to finance more than we paid for the properties. Today, this is considered unethical and is one of the reasons the S&Ls failed at that time. None of my real estate projects ever defaulted or were ever late on a payment.

Back in the Military & Hired by United Airlines

One Sunday afternoon, while answering phones at my real estate office, an Air Force Reserve Colonel from the Selfridge Air Force Reserve Base called to offer me a position flying C-130s. He had found my name on a computer list that showed my clean record, and that I was only eight years short of a military retirement. Although Selfridge was about a two-hour drive north, I jumped at the chance because while real estate brought me success, flying was my true passion. I initially wasn't impressed with the slow, loud and vibrating C-130 A model, but over time I learned to love the airplane and the men and women of the 63rd Tactical Airlift Squadron. After a few years, I was flying as an Aircraft Commander.

Other than the threat of being court-martialed for illegally having an Active Duty green ID card in my possession while being on Reserve status, things went smoothly during my stint in the Air Force Reserves. The green card I mentioned previously in which I was 5'5" and 112 pounds was my first-issued Military ID card, and I had never turned it in after getting off active duty 17 years prior. When I was accidentally caught with it and a high-up General got wind of the event, he assumed I was illegally using it to buy liquor at the base Class 6 Store and groceries at the commissary. Little did he know that I did all my drinking and eating at the Officers Club. Records proved me innocent, but the General still wanted to make an example out of me and demanded that the Squadron Commander issue me an Article 15, which is a reprimand less serious than a Court Martial and more serious than a letter of reprimand.

I originally refused the Article 15 and demanded a Court Martial Trial. I was due a promotion from Captain to Major and I needed the promotion to get 20 years of service to be eligible for a military pension. The Article 15 would have prevented me from being promoted. The Squadron Commander knew I was serious, and he also knew I would most likely be found not guilty in a lengthy Court Marital trial. To save face, he offered me a deal. He would issue an Article 15 against me to make the determined General happy. Once the General saw it in my file, the Commander would destroy all evidence of it, thus making me eligible for promotion. To my knowledge, I was the only officer in the history of the United States Military to be promoted after receiving an Article 15.

A year later, in 1984, I completed the Series 7 and Series 63 testing to become a Licensed Securities Advisor. I placed my securities license with Continental Capital in Sylvania, Ohio. Their habits were like that of the high-flying fraudulent real estate company that I had worked for a few years previous, except their founder was sent to prison. Once again, I was oblivious to the illegal activities that were taking place while I was on staff there.

With boundless cocaine-induced energy, I pressed on and became the active Real Estate Broker for the largest building company in northwest Ohio. I was managing five partnerships, flying for the Air Force Reserves, and was helping raise two sons. During this time, I was drinking daily and using cocaine several days a week. Since I was high functioning, I was convinced that it wasn't hurting me and I could quit at any time. Besides, getting high took the focus away from my failing marriage.

As if I didn't have enough on my plate, in 1986, United Airlines hired me. I knew I had to quit cocaine because the airlines were drug testing. Before I went to Denver to train for United, I endured one last deployment to Panama with the Air Force Reserves. Wanting one last run with cocaine, I snuck off Howard AFB to roam the streets and back alleys in downtown Panama City for a fix. I was willing to risk everything - including my life. I stayed out all night searching for a drug dealer. Thank God, I never found one, and I'm even more grateful that I wasn't stabbed while stumbling around in a drunken stupor that shameful evening. Soon after starting with United Air Lines, my marriage ended. Though I took a break from using cocaine, I quickly filled the void with increased alcohol consumption.

I retired as a Major from the Air Force Reserves in 1991 and built a new home in Sylvania, Ohio, so I could be close to my sons. During the following several years, I had several disastrous relationships, and each time failed to see that I was the problem. I sought lower companionship and alienated the people who loved me. No matter how much I worked, drank, or gambled, nothing could fill the void in my heart.

Hitting Bottom

I continued to fill my body with alcohol and my head with resentments and self-pity. Failed relationships and my lack of self-worth were intensified by my insatiable need to be loved. I longed for good friends, but was incapable of being a friend. The booze had long since stopped working and there was only one thing that could ease my pain – cocaine.

The race to full-blown drug addiction was on. I then advanced to smoking crack, which immediately extinguished any hope of returning to normalcy. I was morally, emotionally, and spiritually dead.

I was well-connected in the drug world and had access to the best drugs around. My main drug dealer called me Ironman because of the large quantities of cocaine I could ingest in a single setting. I would use cocaine to get high and booze to bring me down. I thought I was hiding my behavior from my sons, but I wasn't. For years, my brain lied to me and told me that I didn't have a problem. I destroyed every healthy relationship in my life, ultimately costing me the respect of my sons. For me, the truth about alcohol and drugs is that they robbed me of everything decent in my life. I could not look in the mirror without screaming at myself over what a piece of shit I had become. I would slap the side of my face so hard that on several occasions I gave myself black eyes. I hated myself and I had no idea what to do. I believed to my core that I was unique and that AA or rehab would not help. Eventually, I accepted that I was going to die from my addiction.

People who suffer from drug addiction follow a progressive road to utter destruction. My addiction to booze, cocaine and obsessive thinking brought me to a despicable bottom which I thought would undoubtedly end in death.

God's Intervention and a Profound Moment of Clarity

There is a saying, "God does for us what we can't do for ourselves." What happened next changed everything in my life forever, everything I believed in and everything I was attached to.

The evening of February 3, 1999, started out like many other evenings. I had a fully stocked liquor cabinet, a fridge full of beer, and my drug dealer had dropped off four grams of high-quality cocaine. He only serviced professionals and never cut the drugs. Like Domino's Pizza, he promised delivery in 30 minutes or less or you received a free gram. His motto was, "I may doze, but I never close." I filled the large Jacuzzi tub in my bedroom, unwrapped a Cuban cigar, and poured a snifter of cognac to dip the cigar in. I cooked a small amount of the cocaine so I could smoke it. Wrapping a towel around my body, I went to fetch a beer out of the refrigerator when I noticed some movement from outside the dining room window. Knowing I suffered from drug-induced paranoia, I blew it off, thinking my brain was tricking me again.

Suddenly, BOOM! My front door blew off its hinges and hit the floor. Splinters from the doorjamb came down like confetti all over the foyer. What seemed like a dozen men in black ski masks carrying shotguns, hand guns and riot batons came running directly at me, knocking me to the floor, stripping me of my towel.

I had experienced premonitions about being busted, but I never imagined myself like this: naked and shivering, face-down on my cold kitchen floor with the business end of a cop's shotgun pointed at the back of my head. The denial, fear, pain and embarrassment were almost more than I could take. I suddenly experienced an overwhelming moment of clarity. Looking up the barrel of the shotgun into the steely eyes of the masked narcotics agent, I uttered the most surprising words that marked the turning point of my life: "I'm glad you're here." Strangely, the voice didn't sound like my voice; it was a quiet and calm. I now know whose voice was speaking through me.

Two days later, on February 5, at 1:30 p.m., I trudged out of the Lucas County jail. I hadn't showered or shaved for several days. My mind was spinning with questions and uncertainty. Local TV reporters and their cameramen confronted me. It felt like an attack, and I was not in the mood to chat. They recorded footage of me almost punching a reporter who stuck a microphone in my face.

Once home, I received a call from my chief pilot, Captain Gary Meermans, from LAX. He had received news in California of my arrest and, to my disbelief, he asked me if I wanted help for my addiction. He denied that he was calling to fire me, which was what I expected and felt I deserved. He had already arranged for me to go to treatment at Fireside Hospital in Sandusky, Ohio. Although his words were comforting, I thought they were meaningless because I believed I was headed for prison. I agreed to go treatment but was dumbfounded when he said I needed to go right away because they were holding a bed for me. Still, I said OK and informed my family of the plan.

It was just after 3 p.m. and my sons were just being let out of school. I called them and said I needed them to come over right away. That confrontation was the most humiliating experience of my life. I was face to face with my sons explaining that I had been arrested for possession of drugs, and that I was going to be on the evening news. Nathan, 19, and Lucas, 17, witnessed my shame and, out of compassion, pretended not to be upset. Still, I could see their pain. I was aware of the embarrassment that was soon to follow for them.

Before my father left my house, he said to me, "Go get help for the stuff you've been putting up your nose and when you get home we'll just drink beer together." I agreed. I was oblivious to anything having to do with sobriety and recovery. The idea of total abstinence was foreign to me. I had no idea what the journey ahead would bring. I only knew that I had to change my behavior and my thinking. My old way of living was over and I had no clue about how to live without getting high. That was February 5, 1999, and I have been clean and sober ever since.

There were 21 local TV segments on my arrest and arraignment. My arrest was the lead story on the news for several nights as the media and the police continually reported exaggerated details of the event. Some of the wonderful people from my hometown of Deshler started a prayer group on my behalf. There were TV broadcasts from in front of my home where the drug bust took place, revealing my address to the public. Yet, I did not receive one negative letter or phone call. To my surprise, I received many letters and calls of support.

Rehab - Treatment for a Self-Induced Neurological Disease

I spent ten days at Fireside Hospital in Sandusky, Ohio, detoxifying from the drugs and alcohol. The intake nurse left the room after completing my assessment. Of course, I wanted to see what she had written. As I read her medical and physical assessment, I began to feel sick to my stomach. She pointed out my tremors, but most humiliating, she noted the disgusting black scum under my fingernails that is apparent in most crackheads because they constantly scrape their crack pipes and other paraphernalia to get residue to re-smoke for one last little high. How disgusting!

She suggested that I read a book by Terry Gorski, and watch Father Martin videos instead of watching TV that contained continued news releases of my arrest. Detoxifying my shriveled body was painful and nauseating, however I gained 16 pounds in my short stay at Fireside.

It was suggested by my company's employee assistance program (EAP) that I change rehab programs. They wanted me to get out of Ohio and attend treatment away from home. I flew into LAX and on February 22, 1999, from where my youngest sister, Lois, drove me to Cornerstone Treatment Center in

Tustin, California. Lois was the major reason I had chosen Southern California for inpatient treatment, as she had already achieved seven years of sobriety. Having Lois' support nearby was very beneficial.

The first person I met at Cornerstone was the intake coordinator and counselor, Nora Metcalf. It was obvious to my still narcissistic mind that Nora didn't know who I was, as she insisted on treating me like everyone else. She didn't seem to like me much and the feeling was mutual.

My first obstacle in recovery was accepting that I wasn't unique. I discovered that my legal woes were small compared to most. I also learned that my past pathetic behavior was quite typical for a crackhead, a name my counselor John Patty (aka, King John) gave me because of my insistence that since I cooked my own cocaine and avoided street crack, I really wasn't a crackhead.

My perception of God was the first thing that needed to change. I needed to replace the absurdity of trying to understand the mind of God, with the awareness of God's will for me.

I also needed to change how I treated people and myself. I learned that if I wanted to have good friends, I had to be a good friend. I began to understand that pleasure does not bring happiness. To healthy, mature people, these ideas sound basic; however, they are innovative for an egotistical addict.

While attending process groups at Cornerstone, I began to picture myself doing what my counselor was doing. It was much like envisioning taking off in the T-38, remembering the picture I had on my desk years ago. I began to visualize myself guiding people in recovery the way John was guiding me.

On March 24, 1999, I completed the 30-day inpatient treatment and was about to experience my first exposure to the real world since my arrest. Upon release from inpatient, I followed the directions of my exit plan. This meant that my next action was to check into a sober-living home. Lois dropped off an old Nissan truck in front of the Cornerstone facility for me to drive to my new residence. As soon as I drove away from Cornerstone, my first thought was, Larry, there's a 7-Eleven two blocks behind you. You can go toss down a couple beers, rinse with some Listerine, and then go to sober living and no one would ever know the difference.

Whoa! With everything in my life on the line, and 47 days sober, I was still thinking like a fool. I was facing prison along with the loss of my family, career, and health, and still my brain told me to go ahead and drink just one more time. I was fortunate enough to recall something a young man had said the day before: "Just don't act on your craving today. Tell yourself, 'maybe tomorrow but not today'." The thought that I could put off drinking until tomorrow worked in that crucial moment. That was the closest I ever came to relapsing.

On June 22, 1999, when the local Toledo news media finally gave up on attending my court hearings, a brand-new judge to my case granted a Treatment in Lieu of Conviction judgment. This meant that I would not be prosecuted on any of the charges unless I screwed up again. If I did, they would pull this case out of the file and prosecute my charges to the max. I dodged a bullet that could have landed me in prison, and prevented the licensing branch of the FAA from rescinding my pilot licenses, since I had not been convicted of anything. Now, I only had to convince the medical branch of the FAA and the team of professionals monitoring my every move that I was no longer dependent on alcohol and drugs, and that I was mentally fit to fly.

Reinstatement by the FAA

In July of 1999, my Aviation Medical Examiner, my FAA-approved Psychiatrist, the United Airlines EAP representatives, the Airline Pilots Association representatives and the Chief Pilot agreed to submit my paperwork to the FAA, requesting they grant me a Special Issuance Medical Certificate. A six-inch stack of paperwork was sent to the Federal Aviation Administration Headquarters in Washington, D.C. for a complete review. If approved in Washington D.C., it would then be forwarded to the FAA offices in Oklahoma City for further consideration. Several more doctors and psychiatrists would have to determine my fitness to fly and under what conditions they would allow me to get back in the cockpit.

Nine months after being arrested, I strapped into a 747 at San Francisco

International Airport and flew 400 people to Kona, Hawaii. Climbing through 10,000 feet, I looked back at the northern coast of California disappearing behind the wing. I was behind the yoke again. The check pilot that was with me did not know why I was re-qualifying, let alone why there were tears in my eyes.

Before the flight, while completing the flight plan, the check captain received a phone call from the dispatcher. I heard him say, "Alcohol test, you've got to be kidding! We're supposed to push back in 50 minutes!" I thought, Oh boy, here we go – first day back to work and already the Feds are screening me. Instead, he had been randomly selected for a rare random alcohol test. What a God shot! I laughed all the way to the aircraft. The real irony was that this was the only time in my 40 years of aviation that I witnessed any crew member be tested for alcohol before a flight.

On February 5, 2000, I celebrated one year clean and sober at the Alano Club in Newport Beach, California. Nora, the counselor whom I had once despised, presented me with my chip and cake. Nora and I remain friends today. I realize more than ever that her tough love while I was in treatment was exactly what I needed.

I was warned about complacency, and my recovery did stall out after the first year. I had only completed three of the twelve steps. I was gambling and became preoccupied with women. I had gained weight, was using smokeless tobacco, and drinking tons of caffeine. I was replacing the void I missed from cocaine and alcohol with other substances and self-defeating behaviors.

I couldn't figure out why none of the newcomers had asked me to sponsor them. Then, my sponsor pointed out that maybe I didn't have anything that others wanted. I was attending 12-step meetings, but was not engaged in the program. I was taking everyone's inventory except my own.

After another brush with the law, it became apparent that I had slipped into my old self-sabotaging behaviors. My lack of commitment and effort to my recovery had put me in relapse mode. I didn't drink or use, but I was heading in that direction. Once again, agony and discomfort were the motivators for change.

I was on my third sponsor. We completed the fourth step by listing my resentments and writing about my participation in them. I started writing about the things I had done wrong in my life, using the Roman Catholic Seven Deadly Sins as an outline. I had no problem expounding about pride, greed, anger, sloth, lust, gluttony and envy. Fifty-two pages later, I realized I needed to clean up the wreckage of my past. I needed to make verbal, financial, and physical amends to anyone I had hurt that I could contact. I was amazed at how the people I had hurt were so easy to track down. Some appeared in person, and others I could contact on the phone, through the mail, and on the Internet.

As soon as I completed the steps with my sponsor, I was asked to be a sponsor. My sponsee and I started working the steps together, but he soon relapsed and ended up in a high-speed police chase. He spent three years in Corcoran State Penitentiary.

I learned from that experience that I could not help other men if they would not become honest, open-minded and willing. Instead, I learned more about myself by listening and sponsoring other men. My desire to please my sponsor restricted my progress while working the steps with him. By working with others, I became aware that each step of the 12-step recovery process contains a specific spiritual message, and that the goal of the 12-steps is to achieve a spiritual awakening.

I became passionate about dissecting each phrase within each step. I started journaling my thoughts and soon started writing articles and focusing on one step each month. Every twelve-month cycle, I would rewrite the articles about each step, adding new thoughts and deeper spiritual messages. Much of what I wrote is in this book. My hope is that my personal transformation will inspire people, in and out of recovery, to find deeper meaning and purpose in this life in preparation for the next.

Lori – My Wife and Partner

In January 2003, while at a meeting at the Canyon Club in Laguna Beach, my sponsor introduced me to Lori. I found her to be attractive and pleasant, but that was as far as it went. A few weeks later, after the same meeting, she was standing by my car as I made my way to the parking lot. Lori, although an Alumni of Betty Ford, was considered a newcomer and had consumed her last drink on January 18, 2003, just a week before. We got together that week to have dinner. The sponsor hotline lit up like a Christmas tree, as it was highly frowned on that people with four years of sobriety date a newcomer. Her sponsor called my sponsor who called me to question my intentions. I convinced him that I perceived my intentions as honorable – who's to say? With his reluctant approval, Lori and I continued with our friendship and, before long, started seeing each other exclusively. Lori and I, from the beginning of our relationship, shared an unwavering commitment to recovery. After a year, we became certified addiction counselors together and took classes in EEG neural therapy. This is also known as Biofeedback for the brain.

We had become fascinated with the neurological aspects of addiction after hearing "Dr. Drew" Pinsky speak at an EAP luncheon. We became certified as Neurofeedback Practitioners through the Othmer EEG Institute, and we invested in the EEG neurofeedback equipment. Lori practiced as a neurofeedback technician with Dr. Ray Hansink who utilized this form of treatment with adolescences who suffered from ADD and ADHD.

Lori went on to work full-time as an addiction counselor and built an amazing reputation as a no-nonsense counselor. Her direct, consistent yet compassionate approach to addiction counseling has been extremely effective. She was heavily recruited by many South Orange County treatment centers.

As addiction counselors, Lori and I were not pleased with many things we witnessed in residential and hospital treatment programs. Mostly, it was the lack of personal attention given to patients and clients that bothered us. We witnessed that even excellent counselors were unable to make a real difference in an individual addict's or alcoholic's life, only because of their huge caseloads. We noticed most programs spent five to ten times on marketing as they did on pay for their clinical staff. Many used interns to facilitate large groups.

On April 7, 2011, we opened Get Real Recovery Inc. in San Juan Capistrano, CA. We initially provided an Intensive Outpatient Program (IOP) and meaningful Aftercare in small, focused groups. Recognizing that people are hesitant to open up in a large group setting, we created a business model that allows clients to feel comfortable sharing their feelings in small groups and individual therapy. We also provide FAA approved treatment for pilots with substance abuse issues.

Over the next six years, Get Real Recovery grew into a full-service treatment facility. We added detox and residential inpatient homes, and would earn The Joint Commission Accreditation. Each year we help hundreds of addicts, alcoholics and family members find a new life in recovery.

Lori appears to be the perfect partner for me - in life, love, friendship and business. Having looked back at my actions in past relationships, I made the decision early on in this relationship to do the exact opposite as I had done previously. Our relationship is built on honesty and trust. Imagine that – most people intuitively know this formula, but I had to learn it.

You can say we live in a two-story home: she has her story and I have mine.

Time to Make a Difference

In late 2004, I was released from the FAA mandated monitoring. I vowed that I would not cut back on my recovery program. My love of sobriety and recovery grew stronger. After being released, I immediately became a union (ALPA) representative to the United Airlines Employee Assistance Program.

While on the staff as a counselor at Cornerstone, another vision became reality. I now facilitated groups in the same garage I had sat in five years earlier as a client when I envisioned myself doing what my case manager, John, was doing. I loved looking the clients in the eye and telling them that, figuratively and literally, "I was in your seat."

As I started to understand how much the brain was involved in addiction and recovery, I became aware that this knowledge could help relieve the shame associated with addiction. Knowledge is power for the powerless. The neuroscience of addiction reinforces that recovery requires major reprogramming of the brain's neural pathways. This happens when total abstinence from mind-altering chemicals allows the brain to heal and re-regulate its constant electrochemical activity.

Soon, I began developing educational lectures. I discovered I had a knack for speaking, recognizing that my talents were fueled more by passion than by speaking ability. I'm grateful that passion is far more entertaining for audiences than my lecturing ability.

In August of 2009, I spoke at the International Airline Pilots Association's Safety Forum in Washington D.C. The very group of professionals I had embarrassed with my actions ten years previous now allowed me to present on alcoholism, drug addiction and recovery.

To add to our personal, emotional and spiritual growth, Lori and I completed the course in holistic healing offered at the Optimum Health Institute (OHI) in San Diego. Attending OHI was a life changing experience. We have attended four one week sessions over the past 10 years. Through the knowledge and habits we acquired from OHI, we have improved our health and spiritual condition far beyond what I could have imagined possible. We pray and meditate daily, plus we juice and exercise almost daily. Lori is in the final stage of becoming a Reiki Master, and I have been diligently studying A Course in Miracles for the past seven years.

The most important gift that sobriety has given me is that I have regained the respect of my sons. I have made direct amends and continue to make living amends for my past, and we are now closer than ever. We talk openly and honestly about addiction. I have no secrets to hide and no excuses to offer. I have grown emotionally and spiritually from the pain my addiction caused. I am proud of the men Nathan and Lucas have become.

Both Nathan and Lucas have married wonderful women. Nathan and his wife Stephanie work with homeless, abused and addicted people. Recently, they adopted a beautiful baby boy named Micah. Lucas and his wife Sara have brought my two wonderful grandchildren into the world. Logan was born in 2009, and Caroline was born in 2011.

In January 2010, I published a book entitled, Captain Larry Smith's Daily Life Plan Journal, a goal-setting and journaling guide. In the book, I discuss the importance of establishing goals, saying affirmations, instituting personal boundaries and assessing major areas in one's life daily. I was able to get a draft of the book to Dr. Drew Pinsky who happily endorsed it.

Time to move on After 40 Years of Aviation

In January 2014, my career with United Airlines was on the downhill slide. I had some medical issues that prevented me from continuing, but I wanted one last trip. I had become non-qualified and needed a line check, so I requested that my old friend Don Wolfe fly down from San Francisco to fly with me. He jumped at the opportunity to reunite. After almost 40 years since we had flown F-100s together in the Toledo Air Guard, we would be together in the cockpit of a 747-400 on my last flight with the airlines.

We had a wonderful time on a five-day Sydney trip. While hiking the Coogee-Bondi beach trail, we reminisced about our failures and our successes - both personal and professional. The Wolfman was still a man of men and a fighter pilot's fighter pilot. I treasure his friendship.

On January 14, I made my last landing at LAX. It was not my best touchdown, since it seems that my brain retired while we were about 50 feet in the air. I left the airline as I left the military, with no fanfare, just a smile and a wave goodbye. My aviation career is over. A post I made on Facebook sums up my career:

Gratitude

After 40 years in aviation it appears that I'm hanging up my wings. It's been a hell of a ride. I enlisted in the Toledo Air Guard in August 1968 and attended Officer's School and Air Force Pilot Training in 1974. In the military, I flew three trainers, two fighters (F-100, A-7), and two models of the C130. As a commercial pilot, I flew for Braniff and United Airlines and am licensed to fly the Boeing 727, 737,

747, 757, 767 and 777. I accumulated over 21,000 flight hours, including 10,500 on the 747-400 and have endured well over 1000 ocean crossings.

I will now be focusing my time on being CEO of Get Real Recovery Inc. Lori has made our FAA Pilot Monitoring program a huge success.

I will miss the "wonderful working people" at United Airlines. We have endured the wrath of nine moronic management teams, B-Scales, huge pay cuts, loss of pensions, a misguided ESOP and a bankruptcy. For almost three decades, my fellow employees maintained their integrity and were dedicated to providing safe and comfortable air travel. Thank all of you for your friendship, love, and support.

I especially appreciate my sons, family, friends, ALPA, the previous United EAP, and the FAA Medical Doctors who stayed by my side and guided me through the darkness and embarrassment of addiction. You not only saved my career and my life, you gave me a life worth living. Helping others who struggle with alcohol and drug abuse has become my purpose in life.

Mostly, I thank God for 40 years without scratching an airplane, hurting a person, being violated by the FAA, and without failing a proficiency check. I am grateful that God allows me countless opportunities to align my will with His. Without God, my perception of reality was extremely skewed. With God, I have found truth, love, and meaning in this life.

Lessons Learned

What I have learned about life in recovery is contained in the rest of this book. The spiritual quotes were delivered to me after prayer and meditation. I attempted to place these quotes in the appropriate step. The steps blend together as the sheet music to the symphony of life. And yet, what is music to one person's ear may be rubbish to another – we are all different and we are all the same.

The less I want the more content I am. I have changed how I pray. Instead of petitioning God with a list of my wants, I ask only for an understanding of God's will, and power to carry it out. I am certain that God's will for me is abstinence from mind-altering chemicals. I am confident that the path I am on, as a teacher of recovery, is exactly what I am supposed to be doing in my time left in this world. I have found that being calm and quiet is the only way God and the universe can tell me what they want.

More than 18 years after my arrest, I am fully aware of the presence of God in my life. I know now why my voice sounded different when I said to the masked narcotics agent, "I'm glad you're here." It was the voice of my higher self, also known to me as the Holy Spirit. It was the quiet and calm voice that I had separated my human self from during those grandiose years of morbid excesses. It was the voice that went from my subconscious to my conscious in my moment of need - the voice of the Spirit that I have learned to trust, no matter what events life delivers.

The rest of this book is a spiritual journey of transformation.

Introduction
The Four Levels of Transformation

Few of us recognize or appreciate the true power of the human mind; it's unusual for humans to be fully aware of its effect on our daily lives. The mind creates thoughts based on the filtered or unfiltered perceptions that we allow into our consciousness. There are no idle thoughts; each one produces some form of emotion. If our thoughts go unchecked, we continually play the same loop of negative filtering, which becomes ingrained into our psyche.

The laws of cause and effect are always present during transformation; the cause of conflict in the human mind is fear. The effect of conflict is our misconception that we are alone in this world and powerless over our thoughts and actions.

We must realize that the mind is always active, even when we are sleeping. The mind creates thoughts based on the filtered or unfiltered perceptions that we allow into our consciousness. There are no idle thoughts; each one produces some form of emotion. If our thoughts go unchecked, we continually play the same loop of negative filtering which becomes ingrained into our psyche.

Often, we mention the two basic emotions: love and fear. Since fear is derived from a lack of love, the only real remedy for fear is perfect love. The reality of perfect love comes directly from the Spirit and the misconception of fear is conceived from the notion that we have little to no control over our thoughts.

As a parent, my biggest mistake was introducing fear as a basis for learning new skills. I taught my sons to be afraid of new experiences based on my perception of my failures, which were not failures at all, they were simply experiences. We will now venture through the process of transformation with awareness that, at every juncture, love should and eventually will override fear. We always have the choice to choose love over fear, peace over chaos, faith over doubt, and eternity over death.

*****

There is a level beyond the God-consciousness of a spiritual awakening. There is an unconscious state of competence that equates to being on autopilot in God's world. This degree of vigilance requires a willingness to relinquish everything except God's will; this takes a great amount of effort – until it takes no effort at all.

The word unconscious in the context of this writing means awake, but not aware. Step 1 of the 12-Steps uses the phrase "… - and our lives have become unmanageable." The words competence and incompetence equate to manageability and unmanageability over one's life.

*****

The four psychological stages associated with learning a new skill to demonstrate actual phases that occur when learning a new job, an athletic sport or any a new behavior that is not intrinsically inherent to human beings.

Here, we apply the same principles to the levels of transformation that take place in recovery from not only chemical addiction, but also recovery from the self-sabotaging thoughts and behaviors associated with obsessive and negative thinking.

The Four Levels of Transformation

1: Unconscious Incompetence
2: Conscious Incompetence
3: Conscious Competence
4: Unconscious Competence

Level 1: Unconscious Incompetence

Unconscious incompetence is the human state in which there is something woefully wrong with our thinking and behaviors, and either we don't recognize it, or we believe we are not the one with the problem. This is denial in its truest form. Untreated addicts and alcoholics during chaos due to addiction fall into this category. Denial acts as the brain's defense mechanism, preventing us from feeling the pain associated with reality and truth. Consequently, when asking an alcoholic or addict if alcohol or drugs affect his or her quality of life, the person denial will most likely answer "No!" Many will follow up with statements such as, "It's my spouse who has a problem," or, "My job sucks, that's the real problem."

Some forms of denial related to level one-unconscious incompetence are:
<u>Avoidance:</u> Believing there is nothing wrong.
<u>Deflection:</u> Blaming others.
<u>Reflection:</u> Blaming an accuser.
<u>Minimizing:</u> Telling oneself, I'm not that bad.
<u>Rationalization:</u> If you were me…
<u>Uniqueness:</u> I am different…

I think of denial not as a character defect, but only as a defense mechanism. Well-trained therapists are skilled at confronting denial for what it is: the voice of the ego.

Eventually, the consequences of denial, or unconscious incompetence, become too devastating and the problem transfers into conscious awareness. One exception may be people with personality disorders who may have a more difficult time becoming honest enough to get past this stage. This is due to their inability to clearly see the role they play in their dysfunction.

Moments of clarity often propel people into the next level. These moments are usually preceded by events such as a spouse moving out, an accident, being fired from a job, an arrest or the death of a loved one. They may not be ready to take action, but they are no longer oblivious to the fact that they have a problem.

Level 2: Conscious Incompetence

We now have that initial conscious awareness that some facets of life have become unmanageable. Not yet possessing true clarity, the person still behaves incompetently. It is like being lost in the woods without a clue about which direction to walk.

The negative consequences of one's behaviors start to surface here, often like a domino effect. Health issues arise and self-esteem and integrity plummet. The downward slide seems to pick up momentum once a person boards the elevator going down.

Ground Floor: Extreme lows and highs

The ego speaks first and loudest. Planning the next high or cleaning up the wreckage of the last intoxicating event takes priority over living in the present.

First Floor Down: Family

The family knows there's a problem; it has become the proverbial elephant in the room. Upon recognizing the problem, they will usually do one of two things, and neither is correct:

1. *They do nothing,* hoping that the problem will just go away. They fear looking the elephant in the face.
2. *They nag,* making things worse. Nagging increases the addict's stress and adds to his or hers already low self-esteem. In order to numb this pain, he or she drinks or uses, thus continuing the vicious spiral downward.

Families rarely have a clue as to how to deal with a loved one becoming insane right in front of their eyes.

Second Floor Down: Friends

Healthy friends distance themselves from a substance abuser; unhealthy friends are attracted to the insanity of the substance abuser. On this floor, the substance abuser will typically seek lower companionship or totally isolate. Sane friends want nothing to do with the chaos and the drama created by the addicted person.

Third Floor Down: Finances

It's expensive being addicted. The cost of booze and drugs alone should be alarming. The cost of missed opportunities is equally damaging. Poor financial decisions due to compulsive behaviors result in financial turmoil. The costs of legal consequences rise, taking the addict or alcoholic down another floor…

Fourth Floor Down: Legal

Speeding tickets, stop sign violations, reckless driving, driving under the influence and accidents repeatedly place many addicted people in front of a judge. Throw in some domestic violence and trespassing, and even the previously squeaky-clean citizen finds himself making trips to the courthouse. Courtrooms, jails, prisons and mental institutions are full of druggies and boozers.

Fifth Floor Down: Career

This can be a major turning point for the addict who has a career or a good paying job. Addiction tends to make people good at faking it; often, fellow workers do not recognize how sick the substance abuser is.

I was a master deceiver at work and no one ever confronted me or asked me if I had a problem. Despite having an active company Employee Assistance Program (EAP), I chose to avoid those people at all costs. After my arrest for possession and facing the loss of my aviation career, those EAP people became my confidants and teachers in recovery.

Sixth Floor Down: Jails and institutions

These fine facilities are full of untreated addicts and alcoholics. For some, being locked-up is simply an opportunity to dry out before the next run. For others, the loss of freedom is worse than death.

Seventh Floor Down: Death

I ask my clients and patients to picture themselves in a casket. I ask them to think about what will be said at their funeral.

Then, I ask them if they think they will die if they don't accept help for their addictions. More than 80 percent say yes.

My personal bout with conscious incompetence brought me to believe that I was hopeless and I was going to die an addict. My blind uniqueness told me that rehab would not work for me and that AA was for quitters. I totally relate to an addicts or alcoholics who truly believe that they just can't stop. Many die rather than move on to the next phase. A person may be stuck on this level for a long time. The choices have remained the same over time: You can be locked up, covered up or sobered up.

Level 3: Conscious Competence

Becoming aware that we actually have a choice to heal is instrumental in reaching conscious competence. We recognize the need for change; we become consciously aware that we are not alone on life's journey. We find satisfaction in helping others. We now take responsibility for our thoughts and actions.

When we experience conscious competence, we are not only aware of our addiction, we remind ourselves of it every day. People in recovery who have become honest, open-minded and willing are firmly planted in this stage.

Level 3 is represented well in The Promises of Alcoholics Anonymous:

The Promises

If we are painstaking about this phase of our development, we will be amazed before we are halfway through. We are going to know a new freedom and a new happiness. We will not regret the past nor wish to shut the door on it. We will comprehend the word serenity and we will know peace. No matter how far down the scale we have gone, we will see how our experience can benefit others. That feeling of uselessness and self-pity will disappear. We will lose interest in selfish things and gain interest in our fellows. Self-seeking will slip away. Our whole attitude and outlook upon life will change. Fear of people and of economic insecurity will leave us. We will intuitively know how to handle situations, which used to baffle us. We will suddenly realize that God is doing for us what we could not do for ourselves.[2]

These promises are integral to recognizing the actual results of our commitment to sobriety. However, there is still plenty of room for growth after the promises start coming true.

I believe strongly in the 12-step process; nevertheless, one of the complaints from mental health professionals about 12-step programs is that, after achieving long-term sobriety, many 12-steppers tend to dwell on how sick they are. This criticism has some merit. Some people in recovery may be permanently stuck in this phase of their development. This is not a totally bad thing – it beats living chemically dependent on alcohol or drugs.

An example of being stuck in this phase is when a person with more than 20 years of sobriety states that he or she is still powerless over alcohol. That person is comfortable living in the problem. There is a tendency to place too much emphasis on drunk-a-logs and on how pitifully sick they are as opposed to how well we can become by living in the solution.

On the other hand, others continue to move forward in their recovery. They are able to gain self-esteem and maintain humility. These people rarely use negative self-talk when sharing their experience, strength and hope. They possess admirable qualities and have moved through level three of transformation.

When personal growth slows down in level three, conscious competence, recovery becomes more like work. By being satisfied with his or her personal growth, a recovering person will tend to move backward. Instead of an awareness of personal recovery, some believe they are still living in the throes of step one. Some may argue that the first step implies that we never recover from being powerless. I address this issue when I discuss the first step.

Maintaining one's powerlessness is a defensive tactic. At this point in recovery, I prefer to be on the offense. I also choose to accept and experience all the grace that comes my way.

At this phase of development, I suggest you hold your head high and aspire to live on a higher plane than people who have never sunk to the depth of addiction.

There are many great teachers in 12-step programs, however I am not drawn to those who claim they know the truths and all the answers. They tend to sit in meetings repeating the same stories over and over, and continually preach to the newcomers. They are content to remain consciously competent.
Instead, I am drawn to those who continue to seek knowledge and truth. The truth-seekers tend to read, learn, pray, meditate and journal. Whether they know it or not, they aspire to become unconsciously competent.

Level 4: Unconscious Competence

Every person achieving unconscious competence spent a great deal of time in the conscious competence phase. We can only find ourselves in level four by experiencing the repetition required in level three to maintain sobriety. Like miracles, unconscious competence comes to us – we don't go to it. The level of competence equates to being *self-actualized*, the highest level of existence in Maslow's hierarchy of needs.

When we live our lives in the flow of doing what is right without consciously thinking about it, we experience unconscious competence. At this level, prayer, meditation and being of service are part of daily life. The reward is in the service. While living in level four, we do not to take things personally, nor do we cave in under the weight of the ego. This is spiritual recovery in the highest form.

Living life on this level may be the result of any of the following:
1) Having had a spiritual awakening as a result of the 12 steps
2) A profound spiritual experience such as a near-death incident
3) A massive shift in personal values
4) Spontaneous remission from a terminal disease

When we have thoroughly experienced the 12 steps and have had the spiritual awakening referred to in step 12, we will most likely agree with the following premises:

1) Today, alcohol and drugs have no power in our lives. In fact, we rarely think about drinking or using. We have a God of our understanding, the fellowship of a 12-step program, and we work daily on the maintenance of our spiritual well-being. We are unconsciously competent about avoiding people, places and things that are not on our spiritual path.
2) We no longer allow our egos to successfully challenge God's will for us. We do this by utilizing the quiet voice of the Spirit when making decisions.
3) We recognize that these steps are simplified ways for people to digest God's will slowly. God's accomplishments are not gradual, nor do they ever change. With God, time is meaningless because God is eternal.
4) As half-measures avail us nothing when it comes to recovery from addiction, half-measures also avail us nothing when it comes to our willingness to accept God's will.

Here are some suggestions for maintaining unconscious competence. Upon awakening:

1) Read something of a spiritual nature.
2) Meditate on the lesson received from the spiritual reading.
3) Journal on the experience of the meditation. (Journalizing authentic feelings are easier after meditation.)

The time allotted for each step may vary each day. At times, I may only read one paragraph and other times I will read a chapter.

Upon experiencing level four, unconscious competence, our minds are free of the fear and anxiety created by our egos. It is at these times that we are fully in touch with our higher selves. We listen and follow the quiet voice of the Spirit.

We become oblivious to the chaos of the world and we accept that everything is exactly as it is supposed to be.

An In-depth Spiritual Journey Through the Twelve Steps
Taking the First Step: The Transformation Begins Here and Now

Step 1: "We admitted we were powerless over alcohol - and that our lives had become unmanageable."

*****

For many years, my life was unconsciously unmanageable as I displayed the classic forms of denial; I rationalized, minimized and projected the cause of all my problems onto other people until one day, after a four-day binge of cocaine and alcohol, I came face to face with myself in the mirror. As I stared into my eyes, I started screaming obscenities and calling myself every vulgar word that came to mind. My screams turned into tears and I saw myself exactly as I was: a sniveling, pathetic crack-head who was totally addicted to booze and cocaine. I had turned my life's extraordinary blessings into a deep-seated hatred of myself. I cursed God for allowing this to happen to me. No matter what promises I had made to others and myself, I could not stop drinking or using cocaine. As the tears subsided, I wondered how I could end my life and make it look like an accident. Little did I know that I had not yet hit bottom.

*****

Sickness and death are the physical expressions of the fear of awakening. By experiencing the 12 steps, we receive the gift of a spiritual awakening. This gift releases us from the fear, chaos and drama associated with our previous existence. With this gift, we are reborn into a new life in which we finally experience reality. Miracles, awakenings, and reality come to us – we do not go to them. They are blessings we receive by simply aligning our will with God's will.

*****

Admitting powerlessness instills the acceptance of our situation. As we unearth the willingness to surrender, we open the door to change. Seeking courage and surrender once appeared to be contradicting concepts; in recovery, they go hand in hand and start with the first step. Our healing begins with a divine awareness that we are not alone on this worldly journey.

Transforming from a state of unconscious unmanageability (level one) to conscious unmanageability (level two) brings a suffering addict to the proverbial fork in the road. We have finally awakened from our self-induced stupor of ignorance to the acknowledgement that something is dreadfully wrong with the way we are living. Our life is still unmanageable but now we are aware of it.

For most people suffering from addiction, this is the first time they have objectively looked at themselves. The pain and disgust they feel has finally overridden denial and blind arrogance. Admitting unmanageability and surrendering to powerlessness over our lives is truly the first step to transformation. The first of many decisions in recovery starts right here, right now. Sadly, for some, admitting without surrendering is as far as they ever get. They appear to be permanently stuck in a state of conscious incompetence. Some may visualize a new life, but without taking any action, visualization is just another form of hallucination. Surrendering is a *spiritual* lesson that must be internalized in early recovery.

Step one suggests that we are powerless over something: alcohol, drugs, sex, overeating, gambling or shopping. While we had the power to choose the object or objects of our powerlessness, we have become powerless over life itself. The problem does not lie with the drugs, alcohol or food – it lies within us. We are guilty of merely existing in a far too human world, as opposed to living as the divinely spiritual beings that we were created to be. We may suffer from guilt when we acknowledge our past indiscretions, but we can readily forgive ourselves of human mistakes. Simply asking for forgiveness initiates the healing process of guilt. Shame, however, is far more toxic than guilt because it makes us believe something is inherently wrong with us and that we are not worthy of forgiveness.

I have found that most alcoholics and addicts believe they never measured up to the expectations that families, religions and society wrongly placed upon them. To numb the pain of feeling inadequate, they sought and found refuge in alcohol and drugs. People with codependency find refuge in overindulging in different types of self-sabotaging behaviors. They numb their personal pain by directing their attention to the person or people in their lives who, in their minds, are less functional than themselves. Codependents focus on the past which, in turn, destroys the present. They use the past to project the future while ignoring their own need for happiness.

Others may focus on work or strongly held, closed-minded beliefs. These obsessions can result in the same character defects as addiction. Codependency and addiction go hand in hand. Renowned psychiatrist, Doctor Joseph Pursch M.D., has many times reminded me that, "If you scratch an alcoholic, underneath you will find a codependent."

Unmanageability results from certain defects of character that addiction and obsessive thinking create and demand. Defects common in nearly all addicted people include dishonesty, self-centeredness, selfishness, guilt, shame, denial, procrastination and a lack of awareness of reality. Many of these defects of character are our brain's defense mechanisms that protect us from the truth about ourselves. Reality is simply too painful to process. Recovery starts when we stop separating our thoughts from reality.

Our twisted perception that we are unique must be smashed, along with the belief that our addiction to drugs, obsessions and negative thoughts can be eliminated without help. The first word in the first step, "we," was placed there intentionally. Though the initial draft of the 12 steps started with the word "admitted," the alcoholics writing the steps with Bill W. wanted it clearly understood that no one "trudges the road to happy destiny"[3] alone.

In the beginning, the seemingly impossible task of grasping reality appears overwhelming because we have allowed our perception to become so extremely distorted. Chemicals have hijacked our brain and our thoughts. These deceptive and self-destructive thoughts are so pervasive and ingrained that they slowly became our reality. This false reality then creates a sense of comfort until that moment of clarity, that profound instant that we know we are going to die unless we change.

Step one in the book *Twelve Steps and Twelve Traditions*[4] states, "We perceive that only through utter defeat are we able to take our first step toward liberation and strength. Our admissions of personal powerlessness finally turn out to be firm bedrocks upon which happy and purposeful lives can be built."

The 12 steps act as the road map to living life in a world that appears to have no direction and makes no sense. We eventually discover that the world need not make sense once we recover from the hopeless mind-state that we experienced as the result of addiction and codependency. The goal of the 12 steps is to deliver a spiritual awakening, a new life that is a miracle based on truth. Step one is the beginning of the transformation from a broken belief system to a life filled with meaning and purpose.

While we find purpose by redefining our values, they shift gradually in recovery and they tend to differ between men and women. While both men and women find more purpose through spirituality, men place their focus on power, money and pleasure and find purpose in family and personal peace, while women tend to place their focus on independence, family, career and fitting in, and find purpose in personal growth and authentic self-esteem. While these are general observations, the point is that people in recovery, just like people who experience near-death events, will look to find meaning and purpose through repairing their belief systems.

Recovery is not a small heading correction. There is a deadly storm ahead that requires completely reinventing how to experience life from the moment we wake up until we place our head on the pillow each evening. While this seems like an overwhelmingly large task, the seemingly small choices we make in our daily routines determine whether we plow through the storm or we avoid the storm entirely.

We must allow recovery to flow through us and share what we learn when we learn it. As we find fragments of peace on the path of transformation, we must capture that peace and make a home for it in our hearts and souls. This peace comes through internalizing God's omnipotence and omnipresence, and by completely surrendering our will to God's will. We should constantly remind ourselves that God's will is for us to be happy, joyous and free in this world so that we can claim eternal happiness in the next. We have free will during our brief time on earth, but in eternity, God's will is all there is.

The Serenity Prayer

God, grant me the serenity to accept the things I cannot change,
courage to change the things I can, and the wisdom to know the difference.
Living one day at a time; enjoying one moment at a time;
accepting hardship as the pathway to peace.
Taking, as He did, this sinful world as it is, not as I would have it.
Trusting that He will make all things right if I surrender to His will;
that I may be reasonably happy in this life, and supremely happy
with Him forever in the next. Amen.

Hope – The Bridge Between Surrender and Faith

Step 2: "Came to believe that a power greater than ourselves can restore us to sanity."

*****

I had been given many wake-up calls that it was time to surrender and seek help for my alcoholism and drug addiction. About a year before my publicized arrest, I had an incident with the Sylvania Township police. My son, Lucas, was planning to spend a Friday evening with me after he went to a high school basketball game. He usually just walked to my house after school events, as my home was just down the street from his school.

The night before, I got totally wasted on booze and cocaine. I was frustrated when Lucas called and woke me up to ask me to come pick him up and to drive his friend home from the game. I reluctantly agreed. After dropping Eddie off, Lucas and I stopped at a popular Mexican restaurant named Ventura's. We ate some nachos and I tossed down a couple of margaritas. On the drive home, I went through a yellow light as it was turning red and was pulled over for a stoplight violation. Had I kept my big mouth shut that would have been it; however, I needed to argue with the officer that the light was yellow. My overt objection prompted him to give me a field sobriety test – which I failed.

The police drove Lucas to his mother's home (which went over like a lead balloon) as they hauled me to the police station for a breathalyzer. I only blew a .06 BAC, which was .02 below the legal limit. The officer then wanted a blood test. Knowing it would be positive for cocaine, I called my attorney. He informed the officer that the law was that they could only administer one test, and they chose the breathalyzer. My attorney, not aware that I used cocaine, kept questioning me as to why I didn't want to take the blood test. He finally figured it out, and I end up with a reckless operation conviction.

Since the FAA monitors pilot arrests and I already had a DUI on my record, I convinced the ALPA (Pilot Union) attorneys to stave off the FAA from requiring a substance abuse evaluation. I thought I dodged another bullet, when in truth, I had just prolonged the inevitable; the reality was that I was a drunk and a drug addict.

I actually sought help and took $5,000 cash into an outpatient treatment program in Toledo. I announced upon my grand entrance that I wanted them to fix me, and I wanted no record of it. I made up a name and told them that they could never know my real identity. When they told me that wasn't how it works, I arrogantly grabbed my cash and stomped out the door. I remember hearing the counselor say upon my exit, "Pay me now or pay me later!"

After my arrest the following year, I was finally ready to surrender. From surrender came hope; there was a glimmer of hope that someday, somehow, I could become whole and that maybe God would finally smile upon me.

*****

"The Realm of the Spirit is broad, roomy, all inclusive; never exclusive or forbidding to those who earnestly seek". ~*Alcoholics Anonymous*[5]

"Under each cornerstone of fear on which you have erected your insane system of belief, the truth lies hidden." ~*A Course in Miracles T-14.VII.*

"My misdirected desires were self-designed to fill the terms of my perceived worldly needs. Pleasure and stimulation were my highest priorities and I believed them to be requirements. My broken belief system produced an illusion in my mind that I was completely entitled to my egotistical wants. The ego constantly desired another dose of temporary pleasure, whether it was from chemical substances, sexual gratification, a gambling victory or approval from others. But these and other short-term pleasures never brought happiness. In fact, they delivered nothing but misery."

*****

We all want happiness. However, the means through which we seek that happiness is what matters. Authentic happiness is the opposite of what our ego says it is.

Seeking gratification and approval from others blinds us to our real purpose in life and interferes with our ability to actively experience God's love.

I am now aware that, as long as I am attached to human desires and worldly outcomes, I cannot achieve God-consciousness. God-consciousness is not an attachment but a state of awareness derived from living in the present. Faith and belief eventually become attached to our vision, and our previous means that once served the ego now serve the Spirit.

*****

In step one, we admitted powerlessness, which ultimately resulted in our surrender. We waved the white flag of desperation as we moved from the unconscious state of unmanageability (level one) to the conscious state of unmanageability (level two). The wreckage of our past still exists, as does the pain we have caused. Shedding our denial is the first step in the right direction, but it does little to nothing to correct our incompetence and current existence.

In step three, we make a decision to have faith. To get there, step two serves as the bridge of hope between surrender and faith. Step two is a tall order for most alcoholics, addicts and codependents to digest because many have lost faith in the traditional beliefs that they were taught as children. Some never held spiritual beliefs, while others had faith but were unable to conquer the power that alcohol, drugs and obsessive thinking had over them.

I classify hope in two ways: blind hope and authentic hope.

Blind Hope

Blind hope is hope without a plan of action; it is an expectation that something you desire will come to fruition. Since expectations are merely resentments in the making, blind hope has no positive significance. Blind hope does not have a plan. An example of blind hope is the expectation that life is fair.

I think of time as what humans do from conception until death of the body. Time for each of us is a **BARELY** visible speck compared to eternity. Time is not equal or fair, but eternity is as fair as it is real. Blind hope is misdirected time: it has no correlation or relevance to eternity. One might conclude that time is an illusion and eternity is reality.

"Time and eternity are both in your mind, and will conflict until you perceive time solely as a means to regain eternity." ~ACIM[7]

Authentic Hope

Authentic hope has real substance and a foundation based on the experiences of our brothers and sisters before us. Authentic hope has a track record of proven results and provides a plan of action based on those results. There is no mystery in authentic hope – the only requirement is an open mind.

Step two begins with the phrase "came to believe." This is a brilliant way to introduce a power greater than us. "Came to believe" temporarily lets the suffering person off the hook. At that moment, there is no huge commitment to symbols such as God, Divine Intelligence or a Higher Power. This phrase shows us that God is patiently waiting in the wings for us to become honest, open-minded and willing. When we become ready to change, the door to authentic hope will automatically open. This willingness is the primary principle behind 12-Step recovery.

The 12 steps are not the only tools available for finding hope in recovery. Cognitive Behavioral Therapy (CBT) also provides practical aid to the suffering person. CBT is a psychotherapeutic approach that addresses dysfunctional emotions, maladaptive behaviors and cognitive processes through a number of goal-oriented, explicit, systematic procedures. CBT is problem-focused and designed to replace maladaptive coping skills with functional ones. CBT and the 12 steps seek the same goals with similar methods. Think of CBT as providing practicality for spiritual results and the 12 steps as providing spirituality for practical results.

Recovery is a willingness to make profound changes in belief structures, value systems and daily protocol. We must reinvent how we live life from the moment we wake until we place our head on the pillow each evening. In seeking personal growth, we must recognize we are not our thoughts, and by continually examining our thoughts for truth and honesty, we will gradually move toward reality.

Sanity

The definition of insanity has become a cliché - doing the same things over and over and expecting different results. Interestingly, this characterizes the behavior connected to every form of addiction and cognitive distortion. The word sanity is Greek for wholeness. Step two suggests having the belief that a power greater than oneself can restore sanity. Becoming whole is necessary for recovery. Restoring sanity begins to happen when we lose the mental obsession to drink or use. How we become whole is unique to each of us, but the extent to which we truly internalize the meaning of each step determines how quickly we recover from the hopeless, insane state of mind created by addiction and codependency.

Wholeness

I can distinctly remember a moment in my life when I felt whole. I was 12 years old and sleeping in my parent's backyard in the country, with no one around. I was lying on my back for what seemed like hours staring at the black, starlit sky.

On this warm and incredibly quiet, dark evening, I was mesmerized by the enormity of this universe, which I had learned about in science class. The millions of stars glowing in unison instilled feelings of awe and empowerment. I wondered about all the people in history who looked up at the same stars and what they were thinking as they gazed at this collection of heavenly artwork. I was amazed by the universe and felt intimately close to the simplistic God I knew at that time, the God of love and truth, and for those moments of profound peace, I wanted for nothing. This happened to be the same God with whom I later reacquainted myself in recovery.

Some of the individuals with whom I have worked in recovery claim they never felt whole. They say they came out of the womb broken and cannot relate to the peace and comfort I felt sleeping under the stars. I tell them, "You do not need a reference point to experience wholeness; you only need to believe that a power greater than yourself can deliver you to sanity." Those without a reference point to wholeness can undergo an amazing spiritual awakening when the miracle of recovery comes to them. I have experienced my own spiritual awakening and I have witnessed it in others. Nothing is better than to share life's experiences with others on "the road to that happy destiny."[8]

There are many people in recovery who do not wish to seek a Higher Power and avoid the topic of God, but still believe they can find an awakening of some sort while maintaining sobriety. We tend to label ourselves as believers, agonistic or atheist, yet in recovery we alienate no one. Instead, we accept everyone exactly as they are when they come to us. We share our experience, strength and hope so that others might witness our failures and success. We do not preach, we simply teach by example.

Let Go and Let God

The words "came to believe" signify that the 12 steps are a process. The 12 steps are not orders of what not to do, they are positive suggestions of what to do and, when followed, they lead to a spiritual awakening.

To know something, to believe something and to have faith in something are all different thought processes. Faith is a belief that cannot be proven. Faith is not knowledge, nor is it a feeling. Faith is a choice, a decision, and a function of will. For the atheist or agnostic, the term "came to believe" should not be threatening. It reminds us that the steps are suggested actions. At this point, open-mindedness becomes important as we accept the concept that "more will be revealed". For those who suffer from addiction and have lost all faith, the message of the second step has to do with being open-minded enough to recognize that we don't have all the answers. In fact, maybe we should challenge every belief that we hold dear – especially our beliefs about ourselves.

Chemical addiction had caused my belief system to crumble and, subsequently, my faith was shattered. My distorted thinking alienated me from God and my fellow man; I truly had become morally, emotionally and spiritually bankrupt. My low self-esteem was well-hidden under a mask of egotistical arrogance. For me, the second step was an opportunity to get to know myself and my brothers and sisters of this world. Step two provided another chance at a relationship with the God of my understanding which, in turn, taught me the truth about myself.

Religious teachings radically changed my childhood perception of God. Religion taught me that God was a wrathful entity waiting to judge and punish. The God of my understanding gives me free will to do anything I can humanly imagine while He patiently waits for me to align my will with His. I now comprehend that only God's will can prevail, so it is utterly futile to try to force my ego-driven desires onto this world. The Spirit of God is within each of us in the form of a higher self. This is a quiet, consistent voice that opposes those ego-driven thoughts. Ego-driven thoughts speak first and speak loudest, while truthful answers and solutions come from quiet moments of solitude. Prayer, and more importantly mediation, will eventually reveal that God's will is our will.

A Course in Miracles teaches that we are part of God. Understanding this is the ultimate boost to self-esteem that man or woman can enjoy.

Once we are aware that we are the problem, we may allow hope to enter the picture. Hope is a baby step; the courage and determination to take action and the decision to have faith are truly the pivotal traits required to secure long-term sobriety.

The Conscious Decision to Have Faith

Step 3: "Made a decision to turn our will and our lives over to the care of God as we understood Him."

*****

On February 5 at 1:30 p.m., two days after the drug bust, I trudged out of the Lucas County Jail in Toledo, Ohio. I hadn't showered or shaved for several days. My mind was spinning with questions and uncertainty. A local TV reporter and his cameramen confronted me. It felt like an attack and I was not in the mood to chat. Toledo TV's Channel 13 recorded footage of me almost punching a reporter who had shoved a microphone in my face.

Once home, I received a call from my Los Angeles Chief Pilot, Captain Gary Meermans. I assumed he was calling to fire me, so I wanted to make it easy for him. I told him I was sorry for embarrassing him, my fellow pilots and United Airlines, and that I understood the purpose of his call was to terminate my employment, which was what I expected and felt I deserved. Surprisingly, he said he wasn't calling to fire me.

Although his words were comforting, they felt meaningless since I believed I was headed to prison. He asked me if I would consider going to rehab. I said yes, thinking it would be in a week or two. I was dumbfounded when he said I needed to go right away because they were holding a bed for me. I had to complete one grueling task before I left.

It was just after 3 p.m. and my teenage sons would now be out of school. I called them and said I needed them to come over for a talk. It was the most humiliating experience of my life. I was face to face with my sons, explaining to them that their dad had been arrested for possession of drugs and that I was going to be on the evening news. Nathan, 19, and Lucas, 17, witnessed my shame and out of compassion pretended not to be upset. Still, I could see their pain and knew they were embarrassed by the situation I had created.

I made a decision to myself to never hurt my sons again. Little did I know how many more decisions I would have to make before I could begin to mend the pain and damage I had caused to those I loved and who loved me.

*****

"As we start down the road to a new life in recovery, we make many decisions. We make the decision to choose love over fear, peace over chaos, spirit over ego and truth over deception. Faith in nothing is deception. A man who is solely reliant on his own devices, over time, will enter darkness. The decision to follow the well-lit path of truth and God-consciousness generates simplicity and serenity on the journey to eternity.

The goal of this book is to influence the choices we make, not just with the choice to abstain from mind-altering chemicals, but with the choice of awareness to recognize that every decision we make not only affects our lives, but those of everyone around us — we are all connected.

The choices are simple: there are dark choices and there are bright choices. The first is of the self-driven ego and the second is of the Spirit. The first choice brings pleasure in the form of instant gratification that results in chaos and eventual death. The second choice brings peace, true happpiness and an authentic feeling of self-worth.

It seems more apparent today than at any point in time that there are two strong, opposing and diverting forces in the universe. The camouflaged evil forces that endorse hatred and separation are dangerous to mankind. Many fundamentalist religions are abominations. The positive force of Christ-consciousness hides nothing, forgives and loves all, and leads us to salvation.

*****

Step one to transformation hinges upon the willingness to surrender. Step two opens the door to hope. Step three stipulates the necessity for a conscious decision to have faith in something other than self.

The first three steps in any 12-step program are based on these basic premises:
- I have a problem I can't control or fix myself.
- I surrender and totally accept that I am powerless over my problem.
- I believe that I can become whole by making a decision to have faith. For this to occur, I must let go of my will, become aware of God's will, and distance myself from my ego.

The decision to turn our will and life over to the care of God is not made on a whim. It is a well thought out, internalized process. Once the decision is made, we can find freedom through the trust we have instilled in our higher power.

Unconscious Actions, Conscious Awareness and Impulsivity

Unconscious Actions

Much of what occurs within and between us happens unconsciously. We blink 17,000 times a day and our hearts beat 100,000 times a day all without conscious thought or effort. Most internal body functions do not require active decisions to complete. We turn on a light, flush a toilet and start our automobiles without full consciousness of our actions. Some call it muscle memory, which accounts for 90 percent of the actions taken by experienced pilots while flying. The benefit of muscle memory is that it frees up our brains to concentrate on actions that require our focus in the moment.

    Habits are subconscious actions. The habit to look both ways before crossing the street is ingrained in our brains at an early age. Other habits, such as lighting a cigarette or a joint when stressed, grabbing a beer when passing by the refrigerator or popping another painkiller when there's no real pain, are classic and habitual actions of the addicted. There is rarely a decision process involved with using when addiction exists.

Conscious Awareness

Conscious awareness is a process of recognizing what is going on inside and out. Conscious awareness, or a lack thereof, affects every decision we make. Conscious awareness involves seeing and observing our thoughts and recognizing our feelings. As we evolve, we become consciously aware of how our actions and moods affect others. The higher our level of conscious awareness, the closer our perception is to truth and reality.

Conscious awareness allows us to be present with the people and circumstances we face in the moment. Humans tend to ruminate on the past or project thoughts into the future. With addiction, this is another form of denial – denial of the present. Our brains like familiarity, and the past is familiar, as is the worry we carry in our minds of what bad thing could happen next. When not living in the moment, our nemesis, fear, will work its way into our minds via our egos.

In recovery, we teach how to *live in the present*, which comes with many synonyms: God-consciousness, Christ-consciousness or what athletes and musicians refer to as *being in the zone*. Studies have shown that people are the happiest when they are actively engaged in an activity or experiencing a meaningful connection with another human being. Positive psychology calls this "being in the flow."

Conscious awareness functions as a mirror to a dancer: it allows us to see ourselves exactly as we are. As we cultivate awareness, we reflect upon and respond to challenges and opportunities rather than react to them. Conscious awareness is essential to experiencing positive transformation.

Impulsivity

Impulsivity is a strong, unreflective feeling to act on an urge with little or no forethought. This precisely describes the actions of addicts and obsessed people.

Instant gratification for the addict is a way to escape and avoid feelings of fear, guilt, anger or shame. The reward circuits in the brain are lying in wait, ready to be activated. Craving areas of the brain are awakened by deceptive brain messages and cognitive distortion, causing the addict to act impulsively. Addicts truly believe they have no choice in that moment other than to use. The result is powerlessness.

Impulsivity is self-will taking action without a plan. Ego-driven self-will ignores negative consequences, always choosing pleasure before happiness. Free will unfailingly offers us the ability to choose wisely and works best with a quiet mind. Aligning our will with the eternal freedom rendered by God's will is never impulsive, selfish or destructive.

Decision

We make thousands of decisions every day. Most of these decisions appear not to have any real consequences in our lives. However, even the most trivial decisions that we make can potentially have life-and-death results. A decision to sleep in or to take a different way to work may or may not involve us in an accident. A decision to stay in or go out to socialize may create an opportunity to make a new acquaintance that may turn into a best friend or a horrible enemy. Life is a combination of chance and timing that results in destiny.

Where we are at any given moment is a direct result of the culmination of all the decisions we have made in our lives. Often, while facilitating a group, I suggest that everything every one of us has experienced in the past brought us together *right here, right now* and that acceptance of everything *right here, right now* is the key to finding inner peace.

Other people's decisions also have tremendous consequences in our lives. Every decision made by our parents, and even made by our ancestors over thousands of years, came together to bring us into this world; it took trillions of decisions and events to align perfectly for each of us to find our way to this planet.

Most of our decisions are made without meaningful consideration. However, making a decision to turn over our wills and lives to the care of God is the most monumental decision we can make.

The Big Book of Alcoholics Anonymous uses the following phrases to emphasize that we are constantly in the process of turning over our will to the care of a power greater than ourselves:

- Give ourselves completely.
- Decide to go to any length.
- Remember, half-measures avail us of nothing.
- Think well before taking this step.
- Voice it without reservation.
- Abandon ourselves utterly.
- Be entirely ready.
- Ask with complete abandon.
- Take this position sincerely, honestly and humbly.

Herb Kaighan, in his book *Twelve Steps to Spiritual Awakening*, says, "Willingness is the key and grace is the power that turns that key." [9]

Continuing Solution

As life's problems arise, we are continually forced to turn over our will. We seek to be aware that any hesitation to redirect our conscious awareness comes from pride and ego. Ego relies on the past to destroy the present. Ego speaks first and it speaks loudest. This is when faith is critical: trusting that we can get through any situation is paramount, and living in the moment is essential. Recognize that pain is the catalyst to dethroning ego. We need to be as persistent in pursuing recovery as we were in pursuing the chemicals we used to get us here.

Freedom

During addiction, alcoholics and addicts lost the freedom of choice and, therefore, the freedom of decision. They may not admit this loss, but in their state of consciousness they only make one choice consistently, which is the choice to use. Some will insist they have the right to drink, which they obviously do, by the letter of the law; however, they fail to grasp that they forfeit the freedom of choice by exercising that right.

Recovery avails us the freedom to distance ourselves from the hectic world around us, and to consciously be connected with God. We now have the freedom of choice, the freedom to decide between love and fear.

Final Thought

Many people choose to attack the messages within the 12 steps and the basic principles in recovery. There is even a TV commercial for a non-12-step treatment facility that directly slams the 12 steps. The man in the commercial makes a prideful assertion that he was once an addict and now is not. He states that his program is not a 12-step program – his program "really works" – and for $19.95 you can purchase the secrets found only in his book.

I believe the 12 steps can work for anyone and for any addiction. The caveat is that it requires one to be *all in*.

A Course in Miracles counters such attacks: "When you attack, you are denying yourself. You are specifically teaching yourself that you are not what you are. Your denial of reality precludes the acceptance of God's gift, because you have accepted something else in its place. If you understand this is always an attack on truth, and truth is God, you will realize why it is always fearful. If you further recognize that you are part of God, you will understand why it is that you always attack yourself first."[10]

Getting Real by Facing Reality

Step 4: "Made a searching and fearless moral inventory of ourselves."

*****

The day I entered treatment, the detox nurse who was assigned to me quickly picked up that I was a bit entitled. (Actually, I was an entitled prick.) She started playing a little game with me. The next morning, she arrived in my room with a folded slip of paper. "When I leave," she said, "look up the word written on the paper and explain to me what it means tomorrow." The word was grandiose. I played along and provided her the definition the following day. The next morning, I expounded my precise definition only to be greeted with another folded slip of paper with another word hidden inside. This word was *narcissism*. I had no clue why we were playing this silly game. I looked up the word and was ready for her when she came in the next day. She had another slip of paper in her hand. This game went on for several days before I recognized it wasn't a game. When I queried her as to the purpose of the game, her look was far more powerful than words – she was describing me.

Three years later, when I finally started step four, I remembered that nurse. She helped me to understand that my resentments and fears had been buried under my grandiosity and self-centeredness. Taking a thorough inventory of my past and present was a difficult task that I had put off for far too long.

On my quest for a spiritual awakening, the pain of not completing step four had become more burdensome than the pain of digging in deep to find the source of my character defects. My sponsor suggested using the format found in Twelve Steps and Twelve Traditions in which I review, in-depth, the seven deadly sins for my inventory. He also suggested I write out all my resentments and define my role in each one.

*****

"Rigorous self-assessment allows us to veraciously align our perception with reality.

"Please allow me to know what I see, not just to see what I know." ~Herb Kaighan, Twelve Steps to a Spiritual Awakening[11]

"As our spirit evolves on our path to transformation, our resistant egos will persist; we hesitate at every juncture. The ego loves procrastination and stagnation – therefore, we must terminate our egos as our teachers, open our eyes and ears and hold our heads high during this period of personal growth. Our higher selves will comprehend the importance of this process. We will forever look at our brothers and sisters in a new light. Only those who are courageous enough to extensively explore their souls will find true peace."

*****

Taking our personal inventories is not about placing blame, guilt or shame upon ourselves. A personal inventory is about understanding our flaws so that we may change our thoughts, perceptions and behaviors. This step is about unmasking who we truly are so we can clearly reveal our fears, denials and resentments. A fearless moral inventory empowers us to discover the reality of our souls.

There is no greater form of acceptance than to accept ourselves exactly as God created us; first, we must arrive at an acute awareness of who am I?

It is time to acknowledge the quiet spirit that lives within us. Our decision to have faith unleashes the strength we need to face our pasts and the courage to question our perception. Our past mistakes were merely lessons that brought us to where we are now. Some of us are physically imprisoned as a consequence of mistakes, while others have avoided this fate only to be imprisoned by guilt and shame. We must escape this torment to move forward in our transformation. To clear up the wreckage of our past, we must meet reality head-on.

This process creates an authentic awareness of our humanness and our misled ego. Facing reality and letting go of resentments precipitates freedom and facilitates our awakening. We now live on a higher plane where our healing has just begun.

"Today I will recognize where my salvation is. It is in me because its Source is there. It has not left its Source, and so it cannot have left my mind. I will not look for it outside myself. It is not found outside and then brought in. But from within me it will reach beyond, and everything I see will but reflect the light that shines in me and in itself..." ~A Course in Miracles[12]

Fact-Finding and Fact-Facing

Full disclosure involves the good, the bad and the ugly. People in recovery seem to dread this step, and people outside of recovery rarely feel the need to take such courageous actions. The internalized process of understanding and acknowledging, as well as the willingness to change, is the needed foundation on which to build the path to a spiritual awakening.

In step four, we investigate what makes us tick:
- Why and how did we end up an alcoholic or an addict?
- What character defects or shortcomings were involved that allowed us to stray so far from our core values?
- Are our core values based on truth?
- What perceptions about us are real and what perceptions and beliefs are false?

We are encouraged to be fearless when approaching step four. There are many ways to structure this step, but the most important thing is to just do it. Here are some tips.

Use the Books

Chapter five in Alcoholics Anonymous has many suggestions for completing this step four. The fourth step in the Twelve Steps and Twelve Traditions is extremely useful here too. If we get off track, refer to the books. Sponsors should be actively involved in step four as well. There is no right or wrong way to walk through step 4, but I suggest using both books as guidelines. The process I used with my inventory was to start with eight blank sheets of paper. On the top of the first page write the word resentments. On the top of the other seven pages, write each of the seven deadly sins: pride, greed, lust, wrath, gluttony, envy and sloth. This serves as an outline for our complete and fearless inventory.

Resentments

We begin by writing a list of our resentments, past and present. In almost every case, there will be an element of our own wrongdoing attached to each one. So, consider the role we played in the resentment and write it down. Thoroughness is the key to being fearless with awareness about how our actions affected others – both are crucial to the healing process.

The two most common areas of life that harvest resentments are money and sex. In our quest for money and sex, we create many problems. We become people-pleasers or may exhibit intense forms of aggression to get our way. We numb our feelings with food, sex and mind-altering chemicals. By doing so, we lose sight of our core values. We cave into human desires, no longer looking within ourselves for solutions. Instead, we place blame on others for our uncomfortable feelings and distorted emotions.

The purpose of working through and experiencing each step is to have a spiritual awakening as a result of these steps. As our clarity about what is real and what is not real surfaces, our thoughts and behaviors consciously and unconsciously mature.

The *Big Book* sums it up: "We would note the power of resentment far exceeds any conception we had of negative thinking." It's important to be aware that:

- A life that includes deep resentment leads only to futility and unhappiness.
- The hours in which we allow futility and unhappiness in our lives are not worthwhile. Resentments waste our lives.
- Resentments shut us off from the sunlight of the Spirit, thereby preventing the maintenance and growth of a spiritual experience.
- When shadowed from the sunlight of the Spirit, the insanity of alcohol returns; we drink again, and we die.
- Harboring resentments is fatal.

Resentments do more than slow down our recovery; they create a physical poison in our bodies by creating ongoing stress and causing our bodies to release cortisol. Cortisol, a steroid hormone, is supposed to be released by the adrenal gland only in dire situations of high stress. Too much release of this hormone has been linked with increased risk of cancer, heart disease, diabetes and other physical diseases, as well as a strong connection to mental illness. It is often said that a resentment is like drinking poison and expecting the other person to die.

A thorough step four reveals the truth about our pasts and our true natures. For years, I harbored a deep resentment for my ex-wife and I made her the scapegoat for my failures. By dissecting my role in this relationship, it became clear that I was responsible for creating the mistrust and dishonesty that eventually destroyed our marriage. By placing myself in her situation, I could see that her actions were simply protective tactics to ensure her survival.

Soon I could also tie my personal insecurities to my actions. I recognized that my low self-esteem had created a belief that I did not possess the power to hurt people. Since I perceived that I was not worthy of love to begin with, I minimized the fact that my words and actions could cause pain in others. When I would verbally attack another or be passive aggressive toward someone, and they naturally retaliated or became hurt, I came to resent them.

The Seven Deadly Sins

The Twelve Steps and Twelve Traditions uses the seven deadly sins when working step four. By the time, we get to step four, we may have already gone over a detailed list of our shortcomings. A thorough step one may have accomplished this, but if not, we can simply write out every negative consequence of our drinking that we can remember. More will pop into our memories over time. Missing a few consequences is not a problem – just don't conveniently leave out the significant ones.

I suggest using the 20/20 method: write 20 negative consequences of our addiction and 20 good things about ourselves. Then we take that list of negative consequences and go deeper to the source – hence the seven deadly sins. This mental exercise of tying character defects to behavior and identifying the underlying emotions assimilates in both our conscious and unconscious minds.

As the *Twelve Steps and Twelve Traditions* points out, the seven deadly sins are universally recognized as common human failings. Since pride is the source of many of our shortcomings, it is a good place to begin step four.

Tips for writing out step four:
- Go beyond behavior: investigate motives, beliefs and values.
- Write freely without concern of vocabulary, punctuation or spelling.

Look for the following while writing:
  o What motives lie behind our behaviors?
  o Were our behaviors based on a belief?
  o Is that belief true?

- I found that many of my actions were motivated by more than one of the seven deadly sins, so don't limit yourself to just these, they are just a launching point.
- Challenging our personal beliefs and attempting to live by the principles of the fellowship requires rigorous attention to our thoughts and actions.
- Take off the mask and see what's underneath. Recognize what defects were in the past. Recognize the defects that we have improved upon in early recovery.
- Most importantly, note what defects we still cling to. Since step six is about removing all defects of character. Take the opportunity at this stage to become acutely aware of the flaws we want to hold onto, they will require the most effort. For me it was anger. I found comfort in the familiarity of my anger. I used anger to intimidate others to get my way and it gave me a false sense of control.
- This is the time to keep peeling the onion until we get to the core of what makes us tick. The more thorough the inventory, the more freedom we find by completing step four.
- Step five should be completed as soon as the inventory is complete.
- Truly experiencing steps four and five are major accomplishments in the journey to having a spiritual awakening.

A Thought Before Step Five
I will accept atonement for myself.

"Here is the end of choice. For here we come to a decision to accept ourselves as God created us. And what is choice except uncertainty of what we are? There is no doubt that is not rooted here. There is no question but reflects this one. There is no conflict that does not entail the single, simple question, 'What am I?'"
~A Course in Miracles[13]

Rising Above
Ego-Driven Shame

Step 5: "Admitted to God, to ourselves, and to another human being the exact natures of our wrongs."

*****

As a child brought up in the Roman Catholic Church, I went to Confession on Saturday afternoons as a ritual. Every week I would begin the prayer, "Bless me Father, for I have sinned."

The next day at Sunday Mass we would sing, "O Lord I Am Not Worthy" during communion. To me, these actions were constant reminders that no matter how hard I tried and or how enthusiastically I worked, I was never enough, nor was I ever worthy.

Many of us grew up in a shame-based environment and find it difficult to overcome those deeply ingrained feelings of unworthiness. It took the most disgusting experience in my life – my highly-publicized arrest – to make me recognize that God loves me just the way I am.

God loved me as a mischievous little boy, a know-it-all, smart-ass alcoholic teenager, and as a 48-year-old cocaine addict. Because of the science behind DNA, I do not accept the premise that we are all created equally, but I do believe that God loves us all equally.

I now understand that Confession, like step five, is not to lament in remorse about my defects of character. By admitting my wrongdoings to another, I am simply disclosing the events that have prevented me from finding the peace of mind that can be only found by aligning my will with God's will. Sharing the truth about my past is not only humbling, it is the recognition that I must shift my values if I am to fulfill my worldly function to be happy.

*****

Openly admitting the exact nature of our wrongs to another person is a daunting task. Our ego tries to keep us in darkness through separation, shame and fear, and it uses procrastination as an instrument to prevent personal growth. The ego never wants us to look inward, because if we look deeply enough, we may find our higher selves, which would in turn render the ego powerless. With thorough self-assessment, we will become aware that we are as we see our fellow man. We recognize ourselves in each other and our true nature is based on love and truth. We require the two-way flow of energy that can only be found in fellowship.

Fear not; the liberating effect of vulnerability and total honesty carries benefits far beyond a simple feeling of relief – it provides us with a spiritual bond to our Creator and our fellow man. Therein lies sanity. .

****

Rising above ego-driven shame may seem like a strange idea when discussing the process of admitting the exact nature of our wrongs. Nevertheless, completing step five allows us to do just that – rise above the shame and guilt we have carried around far too long.

Step five is a major step on the flight to transformation. Overcoming our fears and previous reluctance to face reality can be accomplished with this action-oriented step.

The truth *will* set us free. Step five is not therapy but it is therapeutic. It is not a conversation, it is a full disclosure and a time to experience real intimacy with another human being. The act of divulging our innermost secrets is a humbling experience; if we are completely comfortable doing it, we are not being thorough enough. Step five is the beginning of the destruction of our self-centered and selfish traits. The reward is that we will possess true awareness of who we really are.

It becomes very important to overcome the fear of sharing our innermost secrets with another person. We choose to rise above our personal discomfort because we have a goal to have a spiritual awakening through these steps.

Overcoming Fear with Forgiveness

What does forgiveness have to do with fear? The ego deems it quite appropriate to use fear to avoid the process of overcoming resentments. Ego insists that we exist in fear, guilt and shame. As our ego-driven resentments fester, so does our fear. Some of us are so familiar with fear and resentments that we find a sick sense of comfort in being afraid and angry. We must learn to redirect the voice of the ego and seek the voice of the higher self, the spirit.

In recovery, we make many decisions. In step three, we made a decision to have faith. Now, we make a decision to forgive. We cannot afford to pick and choose how and whom we forgive. We must completely let go of the toxic grudges and negative thinking that has plagued us for far too long.

Forgiveness is a decision that requires action. We will cover the specific actions in later steps, but for now our goal is to internalize the truth that we never have to live in fear, guilt or shame again. This is different from experiencing these emotions. It is inevitable that we experience a wide range of emotions every day; however, being constantly stuck in the same negative emotions creates a misguided perception that we need to live in fear.

Listen to the spirit within – it speaks in a quiet, honest voice. We aim to make ourselves aware of this still, quiet voice of truth. Our spirits will leap beyond our errors and live in the realm of forgiveness. Forgiveness is the remedy to heal the soul, and faith creates a sense of freedom in the soul that cannot be taken away.

How to Work Through Step 5

Start step five with prayer and meditation. This will help clear our minds from anything other than the tasks at hand. We admit to God first, then to ourselves, the exact natures of our wrongs and the character defects associated with each item on our step four lists.

I suggested that, when doing step four, we use the seven deadly sins as a way to categorize our moral inventories. Most character defects (human traits and flaws) will fall under the categories of pride, wrath, lust, sloth, gluttony, envy and greed. This simplifies and organizes the process of presenting step five and makes it easier for us to discuss, process and put closure on each wrongdoing. It also helps the person who is listening to our step five to stay present.

Usually a sponsor will be the best choice to hear step five. We may decide to use a clergy member or a close friend, but whomever we choose should be 100 percent trustworthy and willing to give us open feedback. People who have completed step five have true empathy for us and will personally understand the courage it takes to expose our innermost secrets.

It is important to allow ourselves enough time to complete step five in one sitting because it is beneficial to process the emotions all at once and then be done with it. Remember, this is the first time we are admitting all our mistakes, defects and resentments out loud – it may take some time to process these feelings and emotions.

Choose an appropriate place that is quiet and private. The last thing we want while experiencing this life-changing event is distraction. Every person who has completed the steps remembers precisely where they completed their step five. I suggest not using a paid medical or mental health professional acting in a professional setting to hear step five. This step requires direct, open and honest feedback, not psychoanalysis.

In his book, *Twelve Steps to a Spiritual Awakening*, Kaighan suggests that once we have finished reading our inventory, we go to page 75 of *Alcoholics Anonymous*. It will ask us to answer a few questions:

- Did we write everything that came to our consciousness about resentments, fear and sex?

- Have we kept any secrets?
- If so, remind ourselves why we are working the steps. Keep focused on the big picture.

This may still seem awkward and embarrassing but to achieve the most healing from this step, it is imperative to reveal everything we can remember.

The Results

Here's what the *Big Book* promises about step five:
"Once we have taken this step, withholding nothing, we are delighted. We can look the world in the eye. We can be alone at perfect peace and ease. Our fears fall from us. We begin to feel the nearness of our Creator. We may have had certain spiritual beliefs, but now we begin to have a spiritual experience. The feeling that the drinking problem has disappeared will often come strongly. We feel we are on the Broad Highway, walking hand in hand with the Spirit of the Universe."[14]

Kaighan also notes that, "It's interesting that you've spent several weeks or months writing out a personal inventory – all about yourself. Now you've spent hours reading out loud – all about yourself. And the *Big Book* proclaims that as a result, you know God better."

Therefore, steps four and five are major predecessors to having a spiritual awakening. Neither step is comfortable to experience; both steps take courage to accomplish. The effort put forth to accomplish these steps makes us aware that pain is the price of admission into a meaningful life. We recognize that the better we know ourselves, the stronger our connection is with God.

What I learned by completing step five is that even though my mistakes, my sins, my fears and my resentments seemed grave, they were typically human. My higher power is privy to my humanness and knows that I am able to rise above my ego-driven self to live on an elevated spiritual plane.

After going to Confession as a child, I would feel a small sense of relief after doing complete penance; however, it was more a ritual than a spiritual experience to me, so I didn't fully realize the benefits of the practice. By the way penance usually consisted of saying five Hail Mary's and three Our Father's. It always seemed strange that an assigned penance was to recite the same prayers I would say daily anyway.

I am grateful today that I lived through my addiction and that I seized the opportunity to accomplish step five. As I trudge the path of recovery, I continue to stumble often. However, through my awareness of the 12 steps, I find the strength that prevents me from reentering the hopeless world of addiction.

ENTIRELY READY FOR CHANGE

Step 6: "Were entirely ready to have God remove all these defects of character."

*****

My dad always said that a job worth doing is worth doing well. Recovery teaches the same principle. If you have made the decision to experience the steps, then do them well. This is what the phrase "were entirely ready" in the beginning of step six means. In sobriety, we learn that half-measures do not bring partial results. "Half-measures avail us nothing," zero, nada. Failure to comprehend this principle is the major contributor to relapse.

I tried for decades to pick and choose when I drank or used. I planned how much I would allow myself to consume in the upcoming episode. The insanity of thinking that I could control my actions after I took the first drink or snorted the first line was proven wrong a thousand times.

Step six was and still is my most difficult step to accomplish because my ego always has some input into my thoughts. My ego still tells me that God's will isn't always truth and that my self-serving plan is better for me than what my higher self tells me to do.

Today I start each day with the thought, *How do I really want to see this day unfold – my way or God's way?* I then visualize the upcoming events of the day and look for ways to be of service to others. On days where certain events can be stressful, I think of what I can do to avoid conflict and chaos. By completing steps four and five, I am aware of what character defects could be triggered in the day ahead.

My ego wants me to believe that I am attached to my defects such as anger, self-centeredness and my need to micromanage every tiny detail of my plan for the day. On those days, I carry the long version of the Serenity Prayer with me to remind me of what I have control over. I might be attached to my defects, but my defects are not attached to me. I can resist selfish acts by listening to the quiet voice of The Spirit.

*****

"I tried to exchange my inheritance from God for the world I see. I focused on pain, illness, loss, age and death. Yet, with eternity we are promised perfect security and complete fulfillment.

When we are ready to remove our human defects of character and become willing to accept our true inheritance, we will be free of the illusions of fear and ego. This allows us to smoothly transform through time into eternity.

With step six, atonement is the principle and healing is the result. Healing comes from the release of fear and the separation from the ego."

*****

Completing steps four and five is usually a huge relief for the recovering person. Most people never complete a moral inventory of their entire lives, let alone openly share all their defects of character with another person.

Initially, I thought steps six and seven would be a cinch compared with the hard work and courage required to complete steps four and five . I was wrong. I found that admitting my defects was far easier than wanting to eliminate them entirely. While step six is not a time-consuming or an external step, it requires an internal willingness to change and to create a personal connection with God. Step six is a reality check of our state of willingness and readiness. It is helpful to remember that God knows all and is on our side when addressing step six.

Identifying Defects

We listed and confessed our known defects in steps four and five. Now we must identify and rectify these and any other defects not mentioned in steps four and five.

The best way to identify defects is to review a list of common human flaws, then ask ourselves which apply to us.

Am I?

Selfish
Self-centered
Self-serving
Self-pitying
Self-loathing
Inferior
Judgmental
Lustful
Angry
Slothful
Denying reality
Deceitful
Superior
Passive
Prideful
Embellishing
Revengeful
Gossiping
Greedy
Materialistic
Jealous
Intolerant
Disrespectful
Insincere
Impatient
Procrastinating
Envious
Aggressive
Ungrateful
Grandiose
Needy
Manipulating/Controlling
Irresponsible
Impulsive

Anger, Impatience and Projecting

Anger

Many times, the defects that we wish to gloss over are the very defects we should target the most. The traits that resonate with many recovering people and their codependent loved ones have to do with anger, impatience and resentfulness.

It is no mystery that the hardest defects to have God remove are the ones most ingrained in our personalities. We are attached to these defects, though – remember – they are not attached to us. We may subconsciously (or consciously) fear that without these traits we would not be able to cope or even survive.

Attachment to anger makes us believe that we can control other people. We think, that if we get angry enough or vulgar enough, we can intimidate people to listen to our demands. However, people strongly oppose being bullied. This is precisely why we initially may try to wield our clever charms before resorting to force to impose our way. If we get what we want, our victory is shallow and meaningless. We feel guilty when awareness of our tactics surfaces into our consciousness. Guilt not processed over time becomes toxic shame. Shame is the ego's favorite tool to destroy our self-worth. Shame is also the total opposite of what God's will is for us.

Impatience

Impatience comes from projecting into the future. It separates us from the joy of the moment. We miss the beauty around us and dull our senses by rushing through life. We rush to work, to school or to pick up the kids, and many times we fail to cease an opportunity to stop and smell the coffee or the roses. We need to seize opportunities to take five minutes of quiet time during the day. We can also focus on enjoying the moment by choosing to be 100 percent in that moment. Eckhart Tolle talks about taking a long time to wash our hands. Feeling the gentle massage of our fingers, hands and wrists. Feeling the warm water as it touches our skin. Smelling the fragrance of the soap and listening to the running water. Washing our hands can be an opportunity to quiet the mind, relax the jaw and take a series of deep belly breaths.

Projecting

Obsessing about and exclusively focusing on what bad thing might happen next totally separates us from the present. I learned the art of worrying during childhood and I thought it served me well for many years. My logic was, if you plan for the worst, you will never be disappointed. Now I recognize this as a form of self-sabotage.

My mother, God rest her soul, was a consummate worrier. She projected far in advance of the impending snowstorm, tornado or, her favorite, the well running dry. For years, she mentioned that the underground well that provided all our delicious water was shallow and that it may run dry soon. Lo and behold, one summer day, the well ran dry. It cost a fair amount of money to dig a deeper well, nevertheless it was accomplished quickly and our family survived on our neighbor's water supply for a few days. This is known as a self-fulfilling prophecy: what you think about, you bring about.

I always believed that she willed that well to run dry and that it would have provided water for several more decades had she not brought up her concern so often. My point is that if we constantly focus on what might happen next, we provide that event with energy and may actually cause it to happen.

This form of quantum thinking can work for us in a constructive way too, and is precisely the reason that positive affirmations are so effective. Since I mentioned my mother, whom I think about every day, I wish to share the story of her passing into the next life.

I was scheduled to fly a Sydney trip on July 9, 2006. My son Lucas called me in California from Ohio the day before the trip. He had just visited my mother in the nursing home and told me she was failing, as he had many times before. My initial response was that this has happened before and she always bounces back. But this time there was something persistent in Lucas' voice.

I used vacation days and dropped my trip. My fiancé Lori and I jumped on the first flight out of Los Angeles that would get us to Ohio. Lori, Lucas, my sister Linda, my niece Jill and her husband Lance went to the nursing home on the day that Mom left us for eternity. There was something quite different about her that day. She was totally at peace and kept looking at the picture she had of herself and my dad that sat on her bedside table. She didn't complain of the pain she was in, nor did she seem to have a worry in the world. Her face was absent of fear for the first time in years.

Mom looked me directly in the eye and patted the bed beside her. The others instinctively left the room as I laid down and wrapped my arms around her. She cracked a few one-liners that got us both laughing through our tears. This was the epitome of extreme happiness and deep sorrow in the same moment. We declared our immense love for each other, but it was more than that. It was the gift of being able to feel, to be in the present, to experience what we all must experience in life – the transformation into the next.

Had I not been a sober man that day, Mom and I would have both missed that meaningful life event. I was her only son and I had brought her much joy and profound sadness in this life. But no matter what had happened, in the end it was all about love.

What Does the *Twelve Steps & Twelve Traditions* Say About Step 6?

"This step is the step that separates the men from the boys… Any person capable of enough willingness and honesty to try repeatedly step 6 on all his faults – without any reservations whatever – has indeed come a long way spiritually."[15]

A few pages later it states that "Self-righteous anger also can be very enjoyable. In a perverse way, we can take satisfaction from the fact that many people annoy us, for it brings a comfortable feeling of superiority". And the last paragraph in this chapter states, "The moment we say, 'No, never!' our minds close against the grace of God. Delay is dangerous and rebellion may be fatal. This is the exact point at which we abandon limited objectives and move toward God's will for us."

"Were ready…"

Step six does not say, "We made ourselves entirely ready;" it says, "Were ready to have God remove all these defects of character." The mystical part of this step is that God removes our defects as He did with our obsessions when we admitted powerlessness in step one. Our part was surrendering, then creating hope and then deciding to have faith (steps one, two and three).

The components of step six – "entirely ready," "have God remove" and "all these defects" – are three distinct and very meaningful phrases. I find that dissecting each step helps us deepen the spiritual meaning of each one.

Preparing to Let Go

A good book about letting go is, *You Are Not Your Brain*, by Jeffrey M. Swartz, M.D. and Rebecca Gladding, M.D. It describes the cognitive distortions created by deceptive brain messages. Addiction creates these messages to deliver inaccurate thoughts to our minds. My definition of a deceptive brain message is a thought, urge or desire that leads to an uncomfortable sensation (negative emotion or craving) that leads to a habitual response (drinking, using, negative self-talk, self-pity, codependent behavior or acting on a character defect).

Like our addictions, our defects are repeated so frequently that we start to believe that we can't change. Nothing is further from the truth. However, it does require awareness of our defects, courage and faith to let go, a willingness to take action to change, and the patience and persistence to repeatedly correct our thinking to prevent sliding back into old behaviors.

Here are some tools to help process those repeated negative thoughts and instincts as they pop up in our daily lives. Using the Six R's repeatedly is essential to reprograming our mind from the negativity and or cravings that will continue to haunt us.

The Six R's

- **Recognize:** There I go again. I am not defined by my thoughts!
- **Re-label:** Is this message true or false? (If it's false, rename it.)
- **Reframe:** Review the content of the thought. Is it *I can't* or *I won't*?
- **Refocus:** Focus on truth and the big picture, then find gratitude.
- **Revalue:** Is there a better course of action? What are the consequences and long-term effects? What outcome is the best, worst or more likely to happen?
- **Repetition:** Make self-enhancing thoughts and actions familiar.

Step 6 Opens the Door to a New Life

Remember with step six, atonement is the principle and healing is the result. Healing is the release of fear and separation from the ego. The process of experiencing steps six and seven provides clarity about our purpose on this planet. We become aware that we are worthy and always have been worthy of happiness. These steps are miraculous and play a major part in transformation.

Once we complete step six…
- We start to find balance in our lives.
- Authentically healthy people begin to populate our world.
- The low self-esteem derived from our overinflated egos is replaced with a new sense of humility that delivers the gift of high self-esteem.
- With a new understanding of tolerance and acceptance, we start to bring out the best in the people around us.
- As our struggles with daily living are put into perspective, we will replace fear with joy.
- We remove the barriers that block us from acceptance, love and peace.

Empowerment Through Vulnerability

Step 7: "Humbly asked Him to remove our shortcomings."
*****

Twenty years in the military taught me that empowerment comes from strength. To most folks, being a fighter pilot is a sign of courage because of the high mortality rate associated with people who fly single-seat supersonic jet fighters. Dog fighting, dropping bombs, air-to-air refueling and flying 550 mph 100 feet off the ground are nothing compared to the courage it takes to be totally vulnerable in this world.

Be careful what you wish for: While working step four, my sin of pride came to the forefront. I always pretended to have self-control and believed I was in charge of my own destiny. God was just a figure in the background that was going to judge me some day. With all the vulnerability and humility that I could muster, I asked God to remove my obsession for alcohol and drugs. That prayer was answered almost immediately. God did not override my free will, though. I was finally willing to change and God simply delivered the miracle of recovery as He has for many others before me. God would gradually rise out of the shadows in my life and become an active, living entity with whom I coexist today. God is the source of all my strength and energy.

*****

There appears to be a delicate balance between doing what is right and doing what we think needs to be done for survival in this chaotic world. yet, there is no need to distribute our efforts between love and fear – all undertakings need only be directed toward the awareness of God's love and knowledge of His will for us.

We spend our lives achieving, struggling and resisting, and still the vessel we live in dies. Life's experiences deliver the wisdom to recognize that our human ambitions are of little worth. By no longer fearing death as we feared life, we are given a glimpse of heaven and an invitation to later cross the threshold into eternity.

With the time I have left here, I will remind myself every day that my true purpose is to learn, love, forgive, heal and teach. I will not project the darkness of my ego, but instead humbly convey the glowing light of God's love.

*****

To humbly ask God to remove our defects, we must muster the courage to erase pride. We do this by discovering the empowerment of vulnerability.

Humility is the opposite of pride, arrogance and self-deception. Self-deception is the sum of the misguided thoughts we learned to believe about ourselves. Some of these beliefs we were taught, and some we incorrectly perceived because our brain defends its primitive desires.

Our egos love to deceive us with false pride and low self-esteem, which outwardly appear to be opposite emotions; nevertheless, they are equals in terms of the damage they cause to our mental health. This is the epitome of self-glorification and the delusion of being worthless.

The ego does not understand humility, mistaking it for self-debasement. Humility consists of accepting our roles as spiritual beings. These include learning, healing, loving, forgiving and teaching.

True humility shuts out the screaming voice of the ego and listens to the quiet voice of the Spirit. Occasionally, the ego is sneaky and may whisper a grotesquely bad idea. Therefore, in early recovery from addiction or other mental health issues, we share our ideas and plans with people we trust. We ask for opinions, pray and listen, and then formalize our plans.

Eventually, emotional maturity enables us to distinguish between the voices allowing us to intuitively know how to handle tough decisions. We learn that the voice of the higher self is the message of truth and love because it is the voice of the Holy Spirit.

Step seven is the beginning of our acceptance of our true function on earth. It is a giant stride toward taking our rightful place in salvation. Asking God to remove our shortcomings is empowering in itself. It is a positive assertion of our right to be saved, and it is an acknowledgment of the power that is given to us to teach others. God wants us to communicate with Him, through the Spirit, on a higher level than the prayers we were taught.

A Course in Miracles teaches that God is not part of us but that we are part of God. This is the reason God gave us free will. For us to complete our communion with God in eternity we must align our will with His. The quest to align our will with God's will is our only assignment on earth.

As human beings, it is impossible for us to comprehend the mind of God. With that said, it is not impossible to clearly see the will of God. For man to think like God is like asking a dog to think like Newton. Dogs cannot perceive gravity any more than humans can perceive the reality of God's mind.

We as mankind mistakenly play God by attempting to precisely control the outcomes of our thoughts and actions, and yet we avoid the one real truth: Everlasting life is reality and time on planet Earth is so short that it is merely an illusion.

We make so many assumptions about God based on the half-truths we learned along the way that we entirely miss out on the meaning of faith which is that, no matter what, it's going to be alright.

Comfort Zone and Connections

When we become vulnerable, we initially feel uncomfortable. How long we spend feeling uncomfortable depends on how familiar we are with taking risks. Risk-takers build immunity to the discomfort associated with trying something new. If we accept these premises, we will agree that vulnerability provides for a sense of delayed gratification – uncomfortable now, content late. Recovery professionals are exposed to many uncomfortable situations. The normal human tendency may be to gloss over or avoid discussing the messy or embarrassing topics with our clients.

This avoidance is a passive form of codependency that addictions counselors must be aware of. Once we delve into sensitive issues, the intimate connection that is establish builds trust. To achieve this connection, the addicted person must become vulnerable and honest.

When discussing relationships, addicts will usually bring up heartache. When discussing connections, they divulge a history of disconnection. Addicts rarely have a strong sense of love and belonging, nor do they feel worthy of having a good life. Getting high temporally cures low self-esteem and numbs feelings of unworthiness. True healers are aware that the basis of recovery is guiding a person to feelings of authentic self-worth using vulnerability to bring about empowerment.

People who have a strong sense of self-worth simply "believe they have a strong sense of love and belonging".[16] They *intuitively* believe they are worthy. A core function of counselors is to instill a sense of worthiness while nullifying the attachment to entitlement. In doing so, we help override feelings of shame, abandonment and fear. This transformation is mandatory for a spiritual awakening to occur.

Shame, Abandonment, Fear and Codependent Relationships

Shame is the belief that we are inherently bad and unworthy of love; it is usually internalized at an early age. Shame digs far deeper into our consciousness than the feeling of intrinsic guilt. Being guilty of making human mistakes carries no long-term baggage. Shame is a deeper fear of disconnection followed by the belief that we are not good enough; disconnection leads to feelings of shame and unworthiness.

Shame and abandonment create deep fears in children that prevent emotional and spiritual development. Codependent and addicted parents who themselves have never matured are unable to set good examples. Codependent parents may be overtly enmeshed; they do not allow their children the dignity to make mistakes, feel pain or create individual thought patterns. Many parents make unreasonable demands on the child, and when the child doesn't measure up, he or she internalizes feelings of unworthiness.

Addicted parents who struggle to maintain good appearances in the midst of their chaotic existence are not capable of healthy parental connections with their children. Many times, children will compensate for their immature parents and take on responsibilities beyond their limits. This not only robs children of their youth, it establishes a sense of abandonment. Abandonment may be as subtle as not being mentally present or as obvious as a parent leaving or dying.

It was painful for me to recognize the fear and pain that my addiction caused my sons. I'm grateful today that I now have the opportunity to openly share these thoughts with my sons and take responsibility for my lack of parenting. We cannot mend pain retroactively, but being vulnerable enough to ask for forgiveness and courageous enough to accept that we may not be forgiven is a key to our spiritual growth.

Recognizing the past for what it is and resisting the temptation to blame others, we emit positive vibrations that not only shed light into our consciousness, but also rub off on those close to us. Today, I take the time to listen to my adult sons.

Liberation and Love

The first step toward liberation is gaining an understanding of where our thoughts and behaviors originated. It is paramount that we learn to love ourselves and to realize that positive self-esteem can only come from within. Sharing and giving to others, while also separating ourselves from the chaotic events of daily living, is the beginning of awareness.

This also allows us to transcend from a place of powerlessness to a place of enlightenment. Fear and love cannot coexist because they act in conflicting ways in our lives. Fear is restrictive, repressive and limiting. Love is expressive, abundant and free-flowing. Fear contracts; love expands. Fear retreats and love forges new pathways. Fear is closed off and stagnant; love is open and vibrant. Because of the reflective nature of our universe, the mindset we most often hold will be mirrored in our experiences and in every person we encounter.

We may hold the misguided belief that it is risky to love because we fear rejection. Vulnerability is the willingness to invest in a relationship that may not work out. Vulnerability is saying *I love you* first. One of the greatest gifts of my recovery was having a male friend who had the courage to tell me he loved me first. He was a Marine, a Vietnam veteran. His vulnerability was the catalyst that boosted my then lacking self-esteem. His words made me feel worthy. Soon, it became easy for me to tell my friends that I loved them.

Humor: Don't Take Yourself Too Seriously

I was recently hypnotized in an attempt to investigate my subconscious. I guess I was hoping to get more in touch with my higher self. My hypnotist records her sessions, so her assessment of my time under was most likely very accurate. There were two strong messages that came out in this session. The first was that I needed to have more fun! The second and more profound message was that I take myself too seriously.

Of course, my wife, who has been telling me this for some time, found it amusing that I had to hear it from a hypnotic state for me to internalize this flaw. When I consciously made myself aware of this trait, I started recognizing it in others. It was like buying a new car then suddenly recognizing how many cars just like yours are on the road. I started thinking the whole world is just too damned serious.

Understanding starts with awareness, and knowing how we see others is how we see ourselves. Being aware of how vulnerable we are and taking risks to share our vulnerability separates us from our ego.

Working Step Seven

There are two ways to accomplish step seven: the quick, easy way or the long, challenging way. I tried both and failed miserably at the quick, easy way. I'm still working on the long, challenging way.

While I was still "out there" (code for being an active alcoholic or addict) I was driven by my self-centered fear, which resulted in irrational grandiosity. As with every addict, my brain produced deceptive messages that resulted in cognitive distortion. Long-term cognitive distortion causes broken belief systems and a false sense of self. I believed that my distorted thoughts were true.

History and Truth

The word humility is derived from the Latin word humus, which means earth: common as dirt and having no particular distinction. The sixteenth-century mystic, the first Saint Theresa of Avila says, "Humility is simple truth". The recognition of the importance of humility in humanity goes back much further.

In the sixth century, St. Benedict articulated certain traits that go hand in hand with humility. Even in the 600s they were giving suggestions 12 at a time:
1. Conscious awareness of the reality of God
2. Avoidance of self-will
3. Following directions

4. Transparency (no secrets)
5. Patience and endurance
6. Acceptance
7. Diminishing self
8. Be one of many
9. Observe silence
10. Practice appropriate decorum
11. Speak gently, restrained and brief
12. Be modest

The Seventh Step Prayer

My Creator, I am now willing that You should have all of me, good and bad. I pray that You now remove from me every single defect of character which stands in the way of my usefulness to You and my fellows. Grant me strength, as I go out from here, to do Your bidding. Amen.

The Joy of Atonement, Reparations and Forgiveness

Step eight: "Made a list of all persons we had harmed, and became willing to make amends to them all."

Step nine: "Made direct amends to such people wherever possible, except when to do so would injure them or others."

*****

In 1997, I refused to pay an attorney for his services because he had inadvertently overcharged me. Not only had I stiffed him, I was full of unjustified righteousness over the issue. While working step nine, I attended a 6:30 a.m. AA meeting while on a visit back to Toledo, Ohio.

Lo and behold, the attorney, who was on my amends list, was at that early morning meeting. He warmly greeted me and immediately reminded me of the debt and the invoices that I had conveniently ignored. I asked him what he felt that I owed him and he said, "$500 would suffice." I told him I would mail him a check. He replied, "I bet you have it on you." I looked in my wallet and I had $504. After throwing a buck into the collection plate, I left the meeting with three bucks and a clear conscience.

*****

"We are now aware that God's love and promise of eternity is more real than the illusion of life itself. We intuitively know that our journeys will reunite us with God, not as servants but as part of Him.

The sun has risen. Our wall of shadows can no longer compete with the brightness of God's light. Nevertheless, our transformation has delivered us to a road that narrows, and the insanity of ego will frequently revisit our human minds. Narrow roads are more difficult to navigate, so the ego will produce conflict and scream, "Go back, go back! This path is too difficult."

We must protect the brightness of the light and shelter our spirits with all our hearts. Be brave as we list those we have harmed and become willing to make amends with them all.

We hold our heads high as we complete the next two steps on our paths to total transformation. The Twelve Promises are just around the corner as well as the new life that many before us have discovered through the steps.

Lastly, we must always remember that every situation, perceived correctly, is an opportunity to heal. Forgiveness is always an opportunity for peace, love and serenity."

A Guided Meditation to start steps eight and nine:
Close your eyes and sit quietly in a chair. Picture a closed mahogany door above your head. Now physically lift a hand above your head and slightly crack open the door. Visualize a narrow beam of light shining through the passageway you created. Now feel the misty burst of fresh air on your face and notice the aroma of lilacs lingering around you. Multiply the warmth of this experience by a trillion and you have not matched even a glimpse of eternity."

*****

We create peace with guided imagery and mini meditations. We also create hope by the experience of living the principles within the 12 steps. As we transform, our faith strengthens. True faith is the awareness that we are part of God. By understanding this non-dualistic existence, we better comprehend the non-importance of this world and the omnipresence of God in the next.

If every person in the world would complete the 12 steps, we would experience a major energy shift toward world peace. All human beings benefit from forgiveness and atonement. However, outside of recovery and religion, most people don't intentionally walk through and benefit from these processes. The *Big Book's* references to the words "all" and "whenever possible" are meant to instill the completeness that is required to have the true spiritual experience of the steps.

Some people outside of recovery associate atonement, restitution, reparations and forgiveness with guilt and shame. For the recovering person, nothing is further from the truth. Steps eight and nine are designed to free us from our past;

we are not responsible for how others respond or react to our amends – it's not our business. Also, we should not expect apologies from others during this process. We are only cleaning our own house.

We must start by forgiving those who have hurt or diminished us. I often hear people say, "I can never forgive this person for what he or she has done to me." Forgiveness may take time; learning to forgive is a process that must be repeated over and over again. We may let go of one resentment only to fill the void with another. So, be aware of the universal law: if we want forgiveness, we must grant forgiveness.

Always remember, we are transforming ourselves from mere human beings to spiritual entities so that we may be granted a spiritual awakening. In this journey, we go far beyond our humanness into the realm of God-consciousness. So, we must clean up the wreckage of our pasts and create a new existence based on honesty, responsibility and discipline.

The completion of steps eight and nine indicates a willingness to take responsibility for the damage we created in our lives. Not only do we take ownership for our misdeeds, we attempt to rectify the harm that we have caused. The spiritual growth earned by cleaning up the wreckage of our past is monumental in our quest for the transformation we seek. Listing those we hurt and the willingness to make amends and restitution to the people and institutions we harmed takes humility and courage.

Alcohol and drugs are but symptoms of our problems. Unmanageability – the spiritual malady, the underlying nature of our problem – requires a spiritual solution. The process of making amends is a spiritual experience. It may be painful, but by now we are aware that the price of admission to a new life is pain.

In his writings, Kaighan uses a key word to describe our wrongs: *diminish*. How did we diminish others?
- Physically
- Financially
- Mentally
- Emotionally
- Spiritually

How did we harm another person's…
- Self-esteem
- Pride
- Ambition
- Security
- Personal relations
- Sexual relations
- Finances

These questions probe deeply into our minds and show us how hurtful we can be toward others. Going forward, we recall how our words and actions have devastated others.

Comprising the list of those we've harmed should be a review of our first step (those we've harmed as our lives became increasingly unmanageable) and our fourth step (what we discovered in our searching and fearless moral inventory). We then add any new transgressions we've made against others since the time we completed step four.

The more detailed we are about the harm we have caused, the more relevant and effective the amend will be. We should be aware that holding a resentiment against someone does not automatically indicate that we owe them an apology any more than gossiping about someone alone requires an amend. The question is, did our words or actions harm the person or diminish them physically, financially, mentally, emotionally or spiritually?

Should we place ourselves on the list?

We have been self-centered long enough and, yes, we recognize the harm we have done to ourselves. The action of self-forgiveness is an important part of the entire spiritual awakening. However, the list referred to in step eight is about people and institutions we have harmed. If you must place yourself on the list, I suggest your name be the last.

The *Twelve Steps and Twelve Traditions* does not specifically address placing ourselves on our list, but the last page of step 8 states that:

"We shall want to hold ourselves to the course of admitting the things we have done, meanwhile forgiving the wrongs done to us, real or fancied. We should avoid extreme judgments, both of ourselves and of others involved. We must not exaggerate our defects or theirs. A quiet, objective view will be our steadfast aim… It is the beginning of the end of isolation from our fellows and from God."[17]

Steps 8 and 9 Require Preparation, Ownership and Courage

Many of us struggled with the fourth and fifth step. Listing and discussing our character defects with our sponsors or spiritual advisors was challenging. We know step nine is just around the corner and we are going to be asked to go face to face with those we harmed. For most, this is a daunting task.

Thorough preparation and much discussion with our sponsors or mentors makes step nine much easier. Taking ownership of our transgressions and sharing the details with those who guide us helps pave the way to completing step nine.

Spiritual teacher Marianne Williamson says about courage:
"Our deepest fear is not that we are inadequate; our deepest fear is that we are powerful beyond measure. It is our light, not our darkness, that most frightens us. We ask ourselves, who am I to be brilliant, gorgeous, talented, fabulous? Actually, who are you not to be? You are a child of God. You're playing small doesn't serve the world. There's nothing enlightened about shrinking so that other people won't feel insecure around you. We are all meant to shine; as children, we do. We were born to make manifest the glory of God that is within us. It's not just in some of us; it's in everyone. And as we let our own light shine, we unconsciously give other people permission to do the same. As we are liberated from our own fear, our presence automatically liberates others."

We learn in recovery that, to be forgiven, we must be willing to forgive. So, it's important to be clear about what forgiveness really is. Forgiveness is *not* to:
- Absolve
- Approve
- Befriend
- Condone
- Deny
- Excuse
- Forget
- Ignore
- Minimize
- Pardon
- Reconcile
- Surrender

- Tolerate

Forgiveness is a decision *to not*:
- Exact revenge
- Fear
- Judge
- Resent
- Retaliate
- Seek compensation

Forgiveness *is* a decision to:
- Release them
- Release ourselves
- Be released

Why forgive?

> "How willing are you to forgive your brother? How much do you desire peace instead of endless strife and misery and pain? These questions are the same, in different form. Forgiveness is your peace, for herein lies the end of separation and the dream of danger and destruction, sin, and death; of madness and of murder, grief and loss. This is the 'sacrifice' salvation asks, and gladly offers peace instead of this." ~*A Course in Miracles*[18]

Although these reparations take innumerable forms, there are some general principles that we may find useful.

> "Reminding ourselves that we have decided to go to any lengths to find a spiritual experience, we ask that we be given strength and direction to do the right thing, no matter what the personal consequences may be. We may lose our position or reputation or face jail, but we are willing. We have to be. We must not shrink at anything." (*Alcoholics Anonymous*, p.79)[19]

Most of us have trouble getting started with step nine. It requires courage and humility to come face to face with those whom we have harmed. Direct amends means taking full ownership of our past indiscretions. This means repairing physical and financial damage when necessary and possible. Those who have gone before us in this journey have shared that in some cases it took years for them to pay for the financial damage they had created.

Here are some questions that may come up for us in the process:
- What if it's impossible to repay the damage?
- What do we do if contacting the person could injure or scare them?
- What if the person we harmed is impossible to find or has died?
- What do we do if making amends could result in us being incarcerated?

Remember that step eight states, "became willing to make amends to them all." The words *became willing* are key to this process. In some cases, the willingness is all that is required in step nine. Some amends may be impossible and others extremely time-consuming. In some cases, we may be justified moving on to step ten before completing all the amends of step nine. Once again, ask for help with this decision. However, we should never fail to contact anyone because of embarrassment, fear or procrastination.

> These quotes set the tone for step nine and were selected to answer common questions that arise when working this step.
> I make amends to those who I have harmed.
> I focus on the actions I have taken that hurt others.
> I pay back debts I owe.
> I apologize.
> I write letters.

> I find time to do and say things that would help heal the damage that I have done.
> I try to bring goodness where previously I had brought discord and destruction. (12Steps.org)

After we have made a list of people we have harmed, have reflected carefully upon each instance and have tried to possess ourselves of the right attitude with which to proceed, we will see that the making of direct amends divides those we should approach into several classes. There will be those who ought to be dealt with just as soon as we become reasonably confident that we can maintain our sobriety. There will be those to whom we can make only partial restitution, lest complete disclosures do them or others more harm than good. There will be other cases where action ought to be deferred, and still others in which, by the very nature of the situation, we shall never be able to make direct personal contact at all (Twelve Steps and Twelve Traditions, p 83). Discussing each amend with our sponsors will give us clarity for the task at hand.

Conflict

In some relationships, unresolved conflict may still exist. We do our part to resolve old conflicts by making amends. We want to step away from further antagonisms and ongoing resentments. In many instances, we will simply go to the person and humbly ask for understanding of past wrongs. Sometimes this will be a joyous occasion when an old friend or relative proves very willing to let go of their bitterness. To go to someone who is hurting from the burn of our misdeeds can be dangerous. Indirect amends may be necessary where direct contact would be unsafe or endanger other people. We can only make our amends to the best of our ability. Try to remember that when we make amends, we are doing it for ourselves.

Instead of feeling guilty and remorseful, we feel relieved from our pasts.
An affirmation for making amends is: "I am willing to keep an open mind and heart while in this process. I will use honesty and integrity at every juncture, and I will absolutely avoid hurting others."

"Forgiveness comes when you give up the hope that you can change the past."
~Oprah Winfrey

*****

I had two distinct experiences while accomplishing step nine. The first I wrote about at the beginning of this chapter – my encounter with the attorney I'd stiffed. The second was in high school. There was a girl who I bullied, even though bullying was uncharacteristic of my personality, and I never understood why I was so mean-spirited to this person. She was number one on my list of people I harmed, and in her case I was totally at fault and had no reason or excuse for my awful behavior. After arriving back in California from paying my ex-attorney and fellow AA member, I decided to search for the girl I harmed in high school. She was not popular then, but I took a shot by joining one of the high school classmate websites to look for her. Lo and behold, she was one of only three members from my high school class who belonged to the site. (We only had 52 students in my graduating class.) I sent her a long, heartfelt email apologizing for being such a jerk. I held nothing back and asked for her forgiveness.

I was blown away when I received her response. Not only did she forgive me, she tried to minimize the harm that I had perpetrated on her. She told of struggles in life after high school and that she had lost two husbands to lung cancer. She joked that she finally chose to marry again, this time to a non-smoker. She shared that things eventually turned out well and that she truly enjoys life. She appreciated hearing from me. We are Facebook friends today and we often joke and chat.

After these two experiences, the rest of my amends were a piece of cake. I continue to make living amends with my family, especially my two sons, who witnessed firsthand the damage I caused because of my chemical addictions.

I testify that step nine is a spiritual experience that I would not have wanted to miss. The *Big Book* states the promises of AA start coming true halfway through this step.

The Promises of Addiction vs. the Promises of AA

After the many years I've spent navigating recovery (in ways positive and negative), I've come up with twelve false promises that addiction presents and contrasted these with the true and hopeful promises of Alcoholics Anonymous. The below does not require enumeration since the promises are already numbered.

1. **Addiction Promise 1:** I have lost my freedom and I am void of happiness.
   AA Promise 1: We are going to know a new freedom and new happiness.

2. **Addiction Promise 2:** I will forever relive the past while trying to ignore the extent of the damage I have caused.
   AA Promise 2: We will not regret the past nor wish to shut the door on it.

3. **Addiction Promise 3:** I will live in chaos and restlessness.
   AA Promise 3: We will comprehend the word serenity and we will know peace.

4. **Addiction Promise 4:** I do not develop emotionally or spirituality

while attached to my addiction. I am amazed at how low I sink while basking in denial and self-pity.

AA Promise 4: No matter how far down the scale we have gone, we will see how our experience can benefit others.

5. **Addiction Promise 5:** I will feel sorry for myself and bask in my misery. I am a victim.
   AA Promise 5: That feeling of uselessness and self-pity will disappear.

6. **Addiction Promise 6:** I will be selfish, self-centered and dishonest.
   AA Promise 6: We will lose interest in selfish things and gain interest in our fellows.

7. **Addiction Promise 7:** I will continue to isolate and put my wants and needs first.
   AA Promise 7: Self-seeking will slip away.

8. **Addiction Promise 8:** My attitude and outlook on life sucks. We are all doomed.
   AA Promise 8: Our whole attitude and outlook upon life will change.

9. **Addiction Promise 9:** I constantly fear that I will never have enough.
   AA Promise 9: Fear of people and of economic insecurity will leave us.

10. **Addiction Promise 10:** I do not trust my decisions and I will distance

myself from reality.
AA Promise 10: We will intuitively know how to handle situations which used to baffle us.

11. **Addiction Promise 11:** I have been a liar for so long that I no longer trust God or myself.
AA Promise 11: We will suddenly realize that God is doing for us what we could not do for ourselves.

12. **Addiction Promise 12:** My addiction is too strong; I will never be free of it.
AA Promise 12: Are these extravagant promises? We think not. They are being fulfilled among us – sometimes quickly, sometimes slowly. They will always materialize if we work for them.

No matter what outward appearance we may give in our addiction, we live alone in fear and isolation. In recovery, we use the words us and we because we are never alone thanks to our fellowship and a higher power.

Accomplishing step nine catapults us into our new role as a mature and responsible person. We gain the respect of others and experience a newfound feeling of confidence. No longer do we cower in fear, because we have faced our demons head-on. We take full responsibility for our actions and we distance ourselves from our past lives.

Merging with the Mind of God
~ Just for Today ~

Step ten: "Continued to take personal inventory and when we were wrong promptly admitted it."

*****

In my first decade of sobriety, I would awaken many mornings with a crow sitting at the foot of the bed squawking, *Larry, you are a loser, you will never measure up. Go back to sleep.* I would then rapidly create self-sabotaging thoughts to reinforce the crow's assumed words: *No one really loves you, you don't have enough money, love, respect or meaning in your life!* Thank God I am now aware that the crow is my self-destructive ego. I have learned to quickly shrug off those mindless untruths and boldly initiate my daily routine, which goes like this:

I begin with the Serenity Prayer as I waddle to the bathroom. I scrape, not brush, my tongue with a spoon to dispel the bacteria that grows rampant in one's mouth during sleep. I brush my teeth, use my water-pick and wash my face with a warm cloth. I then drink eight ounces of room temperature, filtered water and drink another eight ounces of H2O with a tablespoon of Bragg's Raw Unfiltered Organic Apple Cider Vinegar because raw apple cider vinegar is very alkaline and helps boost one's immune system. After this I am not only hydrated, I am also alkalized – both are good things.

Before I let the crazy thoughts re-enter my mind, I grab a couple of spiritual readings and head for a quiet place to read – outdoors is perfect if the weather allows.

I read a sentence, a paragraph or maybe a page or two and try to process an intended message for the day. When the message is clear, I close my eyes and meditate. If my mind drifts off, I gently guide my thoughts back to the message.

I usually have one daily reading for that exact date, and then randomly choose a second reading that I pick on the spot, trusting God to guide me to the precise reading I need for that day. This process never fails to deliver.

I follow the quiet meditation by journaling my thoughts. I am not an inherently creative person; nevertheless, what I put on paper at times surprises me as being quite profound. On occasion, I get inspired to bypass the journal and start typing on the computer. When thoughts rush in faster than I can type, I know for certain these thoughts do not come from my conscious mind, but from the God-consciousness generated during my quiet time with my Creator.

On occasion, I deviate from my routine and my ego reappears with hopeless thoughts, or feelings of arrogance. My ego likes to tell me I am different. When I recognize that I have distanced myself from the Spirit, I invariably find myself frustrated and fearful. Recovery has taught me an important message: I can start my day over at any time.

*****

I can change my mood by lucidly experiencing five minutes alone with the mind of God. My will controls my body and God's Will is my Spirit. I don't have a soul, I am a soul, I have a body. My soul has always been and always will be part of my Creator. By aligning with God's Will, I cannot escape or avoid truth. As a human I am unable to understand the mind of God, however, God's Will is easily to grasped. Prayer, mediation and quiet time will quickly align me with the reality and truth of God's Will.

Sit up straight, close your eyes and breathe only through your nose. Relax your jaw. With every exhale release the tension and toxins that separate you from perfection. After a minute, visualize your mind separating from your body, forming a white mist floating above you. For these brief minutes, allow only one thought: My mind holds only what I think with God.[20] Let each word shine with the meaning that God has given it.

*****

Our strength is determined solely by the maintenance of our spiritual condition, which is best achieved by a daily devotion. Quiet thought and a thorough communion with God each morning prepares us for the 24 hours ahead.
By starting the day this way, we fast track ourselves into step ten. If we could al-

ways remember that nothing needs to come between God's will and our will, we would have no need for a personal inventory. However, we tend to forget that our purpose on this planet is to learn, love, forgive, heal and teach. Instead, our egos will occasionally take over and we can become isolated from our higher power and revert to our old ways.

When this occurs – and it will – do not descend into guilt or shame, as those are products of the ego. Instead, quietly ask God, "What is Thy will for me right now?" The answers will come.

The *Big Book* takes a practical and much-needed approach to plan our days. It states that, "We ask God to direct our thinking, especially asking that it be divorced from self-pity, dishonesty or self-seeking motives." It reiterates that "God gave us brains to use" and "our thought-life will be placed on a much higher plane when our thinking is cleared of wrong motives."

We ask God for inspiration in our thoughts and decisions. For all these suggestions to be effective, though, we must quiet our minds, avoid chaos and struggle, and trust the process of recovery.

During the Day

Living in the present is the key to our survival. There is no past and no future; we only live in the present. We can think of the past or the future, but we can't relive the past or project ourselves into the future.

We can create our own reality by searching for beauty in the smallest of objects. A piece of fruit, a plant, a flower or even a weed can reveal its own special beauty. Pets also are great source of peace and love. Hugging a pet releases oxytocin which reduces stress.

If we project love, healing and forgiveness, everything we see changes. My friend Herb K. states, "You know what you do not know you know." I add, and "You see what you cannot see." God-consciousness allows us to perfectly align our will with God's will. Perfect alignment is a million times easier than picking and choosing what parts of God's will to accept as our own.

This is much like recovery from alcohol and drugs or any other form of compulsivity. It is far easier to maintain total abstinence than to try to limit compulsion.

Breathe

Deep breathing takes conscious effort and is extremely effective in relieving tension. It also relaxes the neck, shoulders and back. Think of how a baby's belly goes in and out as the baby breathes. Mimic this by taking air deep into the stomach; this increases blood flow and oxygen through our systems. Increased oxygen delivered to our brains brings clarity if we are in a fog. Deep breathing counteracts stress immediately, so practice it often.

Begin by breathing in through the nostrils while counting to five, letting the lower abdomen fill with air. Slowly let out the air through pursed lips. Say "in" when breathing in, and "out" when breathing out. With practice, we can increase the lengths of the breaths. In only two minutes, we can change our perception of reality.

A Course in Miracles calls the present moment the "holy instant". I suggest using this affirmation throughout your day:

> This instant is the only time there is. Thanks for this instant, Father. It is now I am redeemed. This instant is the time that You have appointed for Your Son's release and for salvation of the world.

At the End of the Day

Before we go to sleep at night, we take time to review our day. Did we spend our time with the Spirit or with our egos? Did we listen to the quiet voice within? Did we react or did we respond to life's challenges? This review is never meant to cause guilt or shame; it is only a tool for personal growth.

Personal growth delivers emotional maturity. Many adults still live with the attitudes of teenagers. Teenagers have the built-in excuse for selfish behaviors because their frontal lobes have not fully developed, which is why, at times, they lack social and moral consciousness. (This is also why teenagers often take risks that seem insane to an adult.) The reason so many adults fail to emotionally mature is simply because their egos have been their teacher and they have ignored the quiet voice of the spirit.

We recognize the ego has had a good day when our thoughts became distorted and the mind was taken over by deceptive brain messages. A twisted perception of reality is created when our brains lie to us. These messages are void of truth even though our egos insist that our thoughts are always true. By listening to our egos, we become selfish and self-centered. The evening personal inventory has one purpose: to realign our perceptions with reality.

Review the following list daily. It is an inventory not only of our behaviors, but also of our thoughts. Were we…?

- Selfish
- Self-centered
- Dishonest
- Resentful
- Fearful
- Envious
- Prideful

- Lazy
- Lustful

Did we...?
- Minimize
- Maximize
- Rationalize
- Catastrophize

Are we subject to...?
- Overgeneralization
- Black-and-white thinking
- Automatically thinking the worst
- Negative filtering and discounting the positive
- Unrealistic comparisons
- Believing our thoughts are always true
- Denial of reality, in any form

The remainder of step ten has to do with promptly admitting our wrongdoings. We need to immediately recognize our behaviors, thoughts and beliefs. We review our values and elevate the standards to which we hold ourselves. Personal growth should be inventoried the same as wrongdoing, always remembering the goal of experiencing the twelve steps is a spiritual awakening. We ask ourselves, do we wish to have a small awakening or do we want to genuinely experience this world with meaning and purpose? Many people in recovery believe that abstinence from booze and drugs is enough. They end up as dry drunks and usually relapse over time.

As we continue with the steps, the worldly road gets narrower. Our behavioral options in life become fewer and fewer. Nevertheless, the reward of spiritual transformation becomes glaringly obvious: there is no better way to experience life than by having a clear mind that allows for God-Consciousness. Our goal is to "live in time as we will live in eternity: in the holy instant of the present moment."

After the Step

In AA meetings, people often say they are seeking a daily reprieve from their addiction. We also need a daily reprieve from fear and conflict.

Countless times, I have lost my serenity by reacting to outside forces. I conveniently blamed people, places and things for my abrupt change in behavior when I was really reacting to my fear and attraction to chaos. I self-sabotaged my recovery with excuses and blame when what I really needed was to start every day with quiet time with God.

My quiet time revealed that teaching others would heal my deep-seated negativity. As written in Luke 22:19, Christ said, "Do this in memory of me." This quote is an appeal for cooperation from teachers and healers. I can do more on behalf of my own healing by sharing my vulnerability with others as long as I teach the solution of empowerment of mind over ego, light over darkness.

Being an educator of recovery has given me meaning and purpose. I strive to start each day with a vision of how I want my day to unfold. I share affirmations to reinforce the lessons that are gifted through sobriety. My daily affirmations are often simple, such as "I am brave" or "I am an example of God's love", or they can be more sophisticated, such as:

"I am content to be wherever God wishes me to be because I know He is with me."
"I am here to represent my Father who sent me."
"I need not create worry, fear or conflict. All will be made right in eternity."
"Today is my greatest day simply because it is today."

Make Me a Channel of Thy Peace

Step eleven: "Sought through prayer and meditation to improve our conscious contact with God, as we understand Him, praying only for knowledge of His will for us and the power to carry that out."

*****

I used to wonder, if God exists and is so powerful and omnipotent, why would He allow man to go so far astray? If God is perfect love, then why do we have to suffer in this life? Why would God allow the forces of nature to kill, injure and destroy our homes and lives? Why wars, hunger, murder, rape, disease and injustice? Why would a just God give so much to a few, and so little to the masses? I had so many *why's* that I started to doubt the existence of God.

Once I stopped asking why, and made the decision to turn my life over to the care of God, the angst that had once controlled my chaotic life dissipated, and slowly the Spirit transformed my soul.

In this world, we have the option to make choices. One option is making the decision to accept that our ego-driven desires are the opposite of God's will. Everlasting peace is ours only when our wills are identical to God's will.

My sponsor used to reiterate, "You need to find a higher power you can do business with." This didn't mean that we could create a God to fit our desires, it meant we must adjust our perception to the reality of who God really is. If we void ourselves from the noise of false teachers and envision what a perfect God would be, then and only then can we scratch the surface of the true omnipotence of our Creator.

Comprehend the reality of God as perfect love and truth. God created man to share in eternity with Him, not as servants, but as part of Him. For man to rejoin with Him in eternity, we must be as He is. To be part of God in eternity, we must make the perpetual choice to pursue perfect love and truth. God granted us free will to make choices here on earth. As we strive to internalize perfect love and truth, we recognize that more will always be revealed. In this life, we transition from mere humans to the spiritual beings God desires us to be.

Step eleven starts: "Sought through prayer and meditation to improve our conscious contact with God..." God-consciousness is not a theory or idealistic jibber-jabber. God-consciousness is realistic, practical and viable in our daily lives. This direct connection with the Spirit heals us instantly from the petty problems that tend to feel overwhelming. The simple words "Thy will, not mine, be done" will bring some relief if we truly comprehend that the reality of God's will is that we reunite with Him.

The second message in step eleven says, "Praying only for knowledge of His will for us and the power to carry it out." When praying for this knowledge we ask ourselves, "What decision is best for all involved?" This will likely bring about the solution we seek as long as it is based on sound, moral principles and therefore God's will. Praying for knowledge of His will and the power to carry it out requires not only willingness, but it requires strength to take the action needed to achieve His will. God's will is not the answer to a mystery, but an elementary reminder that our purpose in this world is love and service.

By reading more into this message, we can also see that the act of asking for God's help with selfish desires actually reinforce our ego's desire to constantly want more. Frustration, challenges and even pain are part of being human. Our role as humans is to redirect the focus away from humanity and onto the spiritual reality of our purpose.

Our egos drive us to focus on vanity and to compete for silly things like the closest parking space at the mall. We feel a need to compete when competition is not necessary. Our egos tell us that everything in life that is unimportant is important, leaving little time to focus on what is of ultimate importance: God's love. This conundrum creates noise and chaos around us. By experiencing step eleven, we find peace of mind in the natural flow of life.

*****

Many religions profess that God has a plan for us. That is true in the enormous realm of eternity, but God having an exact plan for us in the same world in which we have unaltered free will is a conflicting concept. God grants us infinite possibilities to align with His ultimate plan, but as humans we have free agency to snub God at every turn, and many do. Some would preach that this would anger God and therefore those who snubbed God will be punished. I proclaim we leave it up to God. We are not here to judge. Not only should we not judge, we cannot judge; it's not in our job description.

We are not here forever...

This planet is time-limited. The sun will burn out, or massive climate change will destroy us, or man will simply destroy himself. The simple reality of humankind is that we will not last. Life is serious business, but most take it too seriously, often missing the whole point. We fight and die for a patch of land; we focus on accumulation of wealth and material things. We strive for power and victory in the activities we pursue. More is never enough.

We all sin and we all make mistakes. Think of them as obstacles in our paths to eternity. The God of my understanding is not revengeful or wrathful, but a God of perfect love and truth. Such a God is void of fear, shame and guilt. They do not exist within Him. All negative traits driven by ego are man-made. The only thing antipathetic to God is fear.

Duality: A misguided belief

Healing does not transpire by petitioning God with a list of wants. Duality is implied when we believe we are separate from God. This separation turns our prayers into petitions asking for things that are many times out of the realm of God's will. Since we are an expression of God, we merge with God and become aware that duality is part of the illusion created by a misguided belief system.

Another misguided belief is applying human traits to our perception of God. Some perceive that God's mind is like a human's: revengeful, judgmental and wrathful. This perception leads to the belief that God would have us sacrifice and suffer, as opposed to His intent for us to be happy, joyous and free.

Dr. Kenneth Wapnick, a teacher of the non-dualistic concept of God based on *A Course in Miracles*, puts it this way: "The First Person in the Trinity, the Creator, the Source of all being of life, the Father, Whose Fatherhood is established by the existence of His Son, Christ, the First Cause, Whose Son is His Effect; God's essence is spirit, which is shared with all creation, whose unity is the state of Heaven."

God, Spirituality, Religion and Recovery

In recovery, we may reconnect with the religion of our youth if our experience with religion before addiction was rewarding and meaningful. If we have sad memories or lived through any type of abuse, such as emotional, physical and even sexual trauma, we may still seek a more personal connection with God based on love and truth, not based on fear.

Some fundamentalist religions use fear, guilt and shame to intimidate their flocks into adhering to a specific set of principles. These fear-based, maladapted teachings do not sit well with recovering people and may have contributed to the addiction process in the first place.

Regardless of past experiences, the recovering person usually finds a closer connection to God in recovery. Acceptance that everything is exactly as it should be, as well as living with awareness of the present, heals past wounds and past misconceptions over time.

Meditation: The key element to step eleven

Neurologically, meditation occurs when our brainwaves slow down to the Theta Range, which is between four and eight cycles per second. It is slower than the eight to twelve Hz of the calm Alpha state and slightly faster than the Delta, or sleeping state, of the brain. When a person's brain is in an Alpha-Theta state, the mind is half conscious and half meditative. The brain and the body heal during this time because good hormones, such as oxytocin, release, and stress-driven hormones, such as adrenalin and cortisol, remain dormant.

The *Twelve Steps and Twelve Traditions* states that, "the greatest reward from meditation is the sense of belonging that comes over us. We no longer live in a hostile world. We are no longer lost and frightened and purposeless."[21]

Meditation delivers answers to questions we have not yet asked. It is extremely useful to journal after mediation, since we uncover what we did not know that we know. A good start to any day is to read a spiritual message, meditate on the contents, and journal your feelings.

The Eleventh Step Prayer:

Lord make me a channel of thy peace, that where there is hatred, I may bring love; that where there is wrong, I may bring the spirit of forgiveness; that where there is discord, I may bring harmony; that where there is error, I may bring truth; that where there is doubt, I may bring faith; that where there is despair, I may bring hope; that where there are shadows, I may bring light; that where there is sadness, I may bring joy. Lord, grant that I may seek rather to comfort than to be comforted; to understand, than to be understood; to love, than to be loved. For it is by self-forgetting that one finds. It is by forgiving that one is forgiven. It is by dying that one awakens to Eternal Life. Amen.

"There is no strain in doing God's will as soon as you recognize that it is also your own" ~A Course in Miracles

The jubilation we feel by having a spiritual awakening is void of fear and doubt because we experience it in the moment. The only true thought that one can hold about the past is that it is not here.

Guided Meditation

This guided meditation starts by gently stretching your neck. I suggest this be done with your eyes open and preferably outside. However, as with any spiritual exercise, you create your own atmosphere and use your own personal techniques.

With your eyes open and sitting straight up, focus on the distant horizon. With the jaw relaxed, initiate slow, deep breathing only through your nostrils. Slowly tilt your head backward as you breathe in, timing your breaths to completely fill your stomach with air. Hold for a few seconds and slowly breathe out. Allow your head to reposition and your eyes to refocus on the horizon.

Repeat the process, but turn your head slowly to the left while inhaling, gazing as far left as is comfortable, and hold your breath for a few seconds. Start bringing your head back to center, slowly exhaling your breath again until it is totally expelled and your head is facing forward. Repeat to the right, turning you head as far as possible without straining while inhaling. Hold here, then move back to center while exhaling. Now, breathe in while allowing your head to come down, resting your eyes on the expansion of your belly. Hold a few seconds, then bring it back to center while exhaling.

As you arrive back at center, the rest of the meditation is done with the eyes on the horizon. As the airflow slowly passes into your throat, lungs and stomach, feel the brightness of the sun and visualize a glowing light entering the crown chakra on the top of your head. See the light join the fresh, clean air in your throat, lungs and stomach. The synergy of God's light and the life-sustaining oxygen of the planet bring you into the presence of your Source. Allow these moments with God and the Universe to give you a glimpse of what awaits when this world is behind you and you are at last reunited with your Creator.

*****

Listening and affirmation

Hearing is simply one of the five senses. Listening takes place in a holy moment of God-consciousness. Listening can be experienced through any of our senses, and God's healing may be delivered in an infinite number of forms. Our role is to focus on awareness of unselfish solutions for the situations we face.

Listening does not mean we are waiting for answers. In the silent realm of quiet listening, we create an energy field of intention. That intention is to internalize God's will, which is the absolute answer to every prayer.

Affirmations are a wonderful substitute for prayer. Positive affirmations reinforce what we know God's will to be. Affirmations need not dwell on the condition that needs healing; the affirmation sends a message to the universe that we are whole, and the universe mirrors back the same energy that we put forth.

Affirmations may start with the words I am:
- *Courageous and I speak my voice*
- *At peace with the world around me*
- *Responsible and trustworthy*
- *Intelligent and I apply my wisdom*

RECOGNITION OF TRANSFORMATION

Step twelve: "Having had a spiritual awakening as the result of these steps, we tried to carry this message to alcoholics, and to practice these principles in all our affairs."

*****

I spent three years going to meetings, always wondering when the miracle was going to happen. When are they going to teach me the one quote, the one thought that would protect me from my addictions? At times, I questioned why they kept reading those same twelve steps at every meeting. There must be more!

I would read the third, seventh and eleventh-step prayers every morning. They were comforting in the moment, but then my ego and I would spend the rest of the day together arguing, wishing and hoping my life would get better.

Finally, at one of those meetings, I heard the message, "Life is a symphony and the twelve steps are the sheet music." The roadmap to my recovery had been there on the wall at every meeting I attended. I had ignored that the purpose of the steps was to achieve a goal. The goal of having a spiritual awakening as a result of experiencing the steps would transform me, as it had thousands of alcoholics and addicts before me.

I wasn't the only person in the rooms of AA who didn't recognize that the twelve steps had a purpose other than sobriety. A spiritual awakening, a true transformation, will always come to those who can be honest, open-minded and willing to change.

My spiritual awakening did not strike me like a lightning bolt, nor did it happen while frolicking in nature's beauty. It was a profound moment of clarity that occurred while shaving in front of the mirror. As I looked directly into my own eyes I became acutely aware that the self-hatred and shame that I had carried with me for decades had totally disappeared. I smiled at the glow on my face and the love in my eyes and said out loud, *"I'm OK!"*

I think of that moment often and remind myself where I came from and who I am. I can hold my head high as a man in recovery; I never have to live like I once did. If I ever choose to have one drink or ingest one mind-altering drug, it would play tricks on my mind and I would eventually lose everything. My addiction is always lying in wait for me to falter. However, I also know that with the God of my understanding, the fellowship of AA, and the principles of the twelve steps, I am no longer powerless over alcohol and drugs.

*****

"My sobriety alone brought me nothing. Like a prisoner released from a dungeon, beaten and emaciated, my newfound freedom from alcohol and cocaine did not bring me instant joy. My freedom delivered the question we all must eventually ask ourselves: Who am I?

As I started to learn not what I am but who I am, I recognized that the road to absolute peace continually gets narrower and narrower. When the road was no wider than the blade of a razor's edge, I became aware that I have one omnipotent purpose: total acceptance of God's will.

Accomplishments or labels do not define who I am, nor do organizations, employers or fellowships. The world I see is a percipience of me. How I see myself is how I see the world. My ego wants me to perceive a sickly universal illusion. When it succeeds, I comprehend the world as a fearful, merciless place. When I choose to see the world through happy eyes, I no longer judge my brothers and sisters. I recognize their innocence and simply accept them as they are – just like me.

At the moment of my spiritual awakening, I thought, Finally, God is smiling down at me. Now I know He never stopped smiling; I was simply missing in action. I have become aware that God is not positioned above me; rather, I am part of his creation and therefore I am part of Him.

"It's important to note that my step work did not finish with the completion of the twelve steps; it had just begun and it will never be complete. To keep the positive energy of recovery, we must also give it away. If we do not share our gift of recovery it will dissipate within a relatively short time. The shelf life of our healthy condition depends entirely on us actively carrying the message to those who still suffer.

On the day I got home from jail after my arrest, my chief pilot Captain Gary Meer-

mans called me at my home that had been ransacked by the police. He told me that when I get well I could keep what had happened to me a secret and in a few short years no one would remember that it was me who was arrested for possession of cocaine. Then he said, "On the other hand, if you share this experience, it just might help someone else recognize that they also need help."

In that instant I decided to share my experience with others. Little did I know, that quick and undemanding decision would be the cornerstone of my long-term recovery. Sharing my story was the elementary stage in my life as a healer.

A day does not go by that I don't reach out to another recovering person. This is not a noble act; it's simply what I believe I need to do to maintain the incredible life that I have today.

There are so many people suffering from addiction that initially I was baffled about with whom I should spend my time. The solution presented itself: Do not seek out people who need help; help people who seek it."

*****

Having a spiritual awakening is the accumulation of spiritual experiences as the result of practicing all the steps. The journey we are on provides a sense of emotional sobriety that only people who have experienced a quantum shift in values can truly understand. These are the results of the life-changing events.

Sources of Quantum Shifts in Values

- Near-death experience
- Surviving what is usually a fatal disease or accident
- Making a profound and authentic decision to change
- Having a spiritual experience or a spiritual awakening, as referred to in step twelve

I suggest we all challenge every belief system we hold. This includes religious beliefs, political views, parenting rules, stereotypes, prejudices, general attitudes and outlooks on life and, most importantly, our beliefs pertaining to our own self-worth.

If our belief system is not serving our new personal value structure, it best serves us to change our belief system. The two questions we must ask ourselves are: Is this belief true? Is it *always* true?

The next phase is reinventing how we live our lives by daily practicing self-enhancing behaviors, including:

- Prayer
- Meditation
- Spiritual readings
- 12-Step and self-help groups
- Nutrition
- Exercise
- Affirmations
- Personal boundaries
- Volunteer work
- Visualizations
- Laws of Attraction
- Discipline
- Frugality
- Setting goals
- Journaling
- Self-assessment
- Belly laughing

Carrying the Message

Going forward in our daily lives, we reach out to others who suffer from addiction. We walk through life with the strength of a higher power within us and the fellowship of a twelve-step program surrounding us. With this support, we can handle anything that the world throws our way. We must share the gifts we have received by practicing what we have learned in all areas of our lives.

When it comes to carrying the message, the words "we tried" in step twelve remind us that we are in the action business and are not responsible for results. While working with others, I remind myself that I don't like being told what to do. So, I avoid directives and try to make suggestions based on my experiences, thus allowing the person I'm guiding to figure out his or her own way. New people in recovery are sensitive and do not like to be *should upon*.

Experiences in Meetings

Early in my recovery I attended a speaker meeting where the young woman sharing finished every sentence with "you know". I found myself not listening to her message and counting her *you-knows* instead.

The next day I was talking to an old-timer and complained about my experience, noting that I got nothing out of the meeting. He looked at me in a way that only an AA veteran could and replied, "Sometimes your only purpose is to be a set of eyes and ears for the person who is sharing. It's not always about you." Ouch. His message came through loud and clear. This AA thing isn't all about me. Over the next few years, I witnessed many acts of love, kindness and understanding sitting in AA meeting rooms.

A year later, at a large meeting in Newport Beach, California, a young man was asked to read "How it Works" from *Alcoholics Anonymous*. He accepted the request, but he could barely read. He literally struggled with every word longer than three letters. The meeting leader stood quietly behind him and would whisper to him the words he simply could not interpret. His courage to stand up there for what seemed like eternity and muddle through the entire reading was met with a standing ovation from every person in the room. Many of us had tears in our eyes as he left the podium. I felt a wonderful sense of belonging that evening. I knew then that I was part of something much bigger than myself.

The *Big Book* says about Bill W's experience, simply and personally, "Recovery begins when one alcoholic talks to another alcoholic, sharing experience, strength and hope... One alcoholic could affect another as no non-alcoholic could. It also indicated that strenuous work, one alcoholic with another, was vital to permanent recovery."

It goes on to say about accumulated experience, that "Our very lives as ex-problem-drinkers depend upon our constant thought of others and how we might meet their needs."

The *Big Book* refers to step twelve as the "...foundation stone of your recovery. A kindly act occasionally isn't enough. You have to act the Good Samaritan every day, if need be."

Sponsorship

Kaighan, in his book, *Twelve Steps to Spiritual Awakening*, states, "A sponsor is a person who has what you want and is willing to walk the path of recovery with you. He should be available and really care about you, your life and your recovery."[22]

I suggest that we recognize that sponsorship is not a marriage. We should seek a new sponsor if our sponsor doesn't return calls and is not responsive to our needs. Obviously, if a sponsor relapses or is often in relapse mode, it's time to find another. Remember that the primary purpose of a sponsor is to give guidance through the twelve steps.

I have found it helpful to review all the steps before diving into working them. This should include the recognition that we have a goal in mind – achieving a spiritual awakening – as a result of working all the steps to the best of our abilities.

Our ability to experience the intent of each step is based on our conscious awareness of the task at hand. Please take the time to be thorough with every step. This is not a race – each step truly is a spiritual experience. As a sponsor, it is our responsibility to dissect every word of the twelve steps to ensure that our sponsees truly experience each step. This is the very essence of every twelve-step program.

It's a "We" Program and a "We" Experience

Lessons learned…
We may have started down the path of recovery believing we are truly unique. We may hold on to hopes of being able to drink or use drugs without negative consequences. We had surrendered, made decisions and promises to ourselves only to mentally relapse. After getting a glimpse of recovery, we would go back to thinking that we were in control. We bounced between the sanity of the fellowship and the insanity of our egos.

We struggled with denial and questioned every suggested solution. Some of us would surrender to our powerlessness only to drink and use again. We had failed to be totally honest with ourselves or we simply did not place our recovery first. We eventually learned to ignore our egos and allowed our pain to be our teacher. We not only made a decision to change, we took the action required to implement that change.

The actions we took eventually paid off. We experienced a profound spiritual awakening. We could never have imagined the joy we discovered in our new lives as sober people. The promises of AA started to materialize, and as long as we place others before ourselves, they continue to come true.

Decision-Making after Transformation

"Today I will make no decisions by myself..."
Now that we are reborn through a spiritual awakening that was delivered to us, we face continuous decisions. Most routine daily decisions are made subconsciously and easily, without real thought or struggle. We should not become preoccupied with every move we make. Allowing ourselves to flow with total acceptance prevents us from returning to the chaos we faced when starting this journey.

When we find resistance is strong and dedication is weak, we need not fight ourselves. We find strength by simply revisiting our morning meditation. Morning meditations may include a vision of how we wish the 24 hours ahead of us to unfold – what kind of day do I want? My morning meditations end with the affirmation, Today I will make no decisions by myself. This means that today I choose not to be judgmental of situations that may arise, and I will seek help from God when needed.

Since I ask God for help with my decisions, I must acknowledge that His will includes lessons that I need to learn in preparation for eternity. If I judge situations in front I me, I create confusion, uncertainty and, ultimately, fear.

If I forgot to plan the day or my plan for the day has run amok, I can always revert to this affirmation: "If I make no decisions by myself, this day will be given to me" (A Course in Miracles).[23]

And When All Else Fails…

Since the ego speaks loudest and speaks first, despite our good intentions, our egos may get the best of us. When our judgments of others have created uncertainty that results in fear and anger, we *cry now* what? There is nothing to lose by asking for a different frame of reference. Ask for direction that is Spirit-driven. We will recognize the solution as it is delivered in a quiet voice. God's will of non-judgmental love, peace and truth is always the best resource. God is never the enemy. He patiently waits, seemingly in hiding, for us to make the decision to ask for His guidance and the knowledge to carry out His will.

End of The Transformation.

Author's Favorite Spiritual Messages

"Acceptance that we are spiritual beings having a human experience is the basis to sustaining a spiritual awakening."

Step 1
"Sickness and death are the physical expressions of the fear of awakening. By experiencing the 12 steps, we receive the gift of a spiritual awakening. This gift releases us from the fear, chaos and drama associated with our previous existence. With this gift, we are reborn into a new life in which we finally experience reality. Miracles, awakenings, and reality come to us – we do not go to them. They are blessings we receive by simply aligning our will with God's will."

Step 2
"My misdirected desires were self-designed to fill the terms of my perceived worldly needs. Pleasure and stimulation were my highest priorities and I believed them to be requirements. My broken belief system produced an illusion in my mind that I was completely entitled to my egotistical wants. The ego constantly desired another dose of temporary pleasure, whether it was from chemical substances, sexual gratification, a gambling victory or approval from others. But these and other short-term pleasures never brought happiness. In fact, they delivered nothing but misery."

Step 3
"As we start down the road to a new life in recovery, we make many decisions. We make the decision to choose love over fear, peace over chaos, spirit over ego and truth over deception. Faith in nothing is deception. A man

who is solely reliant on his own devices, over time, will enter darkness. The decision to follow the well-lit path of truth and God-consciousness generates simplicity and serenity on the journey to eternity.

The goal of this book is to influence the choices we make, not just with the choice to abstain from mind-altering chemicals, but with the choice of awareness to recognize that every decision we make not only affects our lives, but those of everyone we know, because we are all connected.

The choices are simple: there are dark choices and there are bright choices. The first is of the self-driven ego and the second is of the Spirit. The first choice brings pleasure in the form of instant gratification that results in chaos and eventual death. The second choice brings peace, true happiness and an authentic feeling of self-worth.

It seems more apparent today than at any point in time that there are two strong, opposing and diverting forces in the universe. The camouflaged evil forces disguised as fundamentalist religions are dangerous to mankind's survival if their goal is to separate, hate and judge, for that is not the role of religion. The positive force of Christ-consciousness hides nothing, forgives and loves all, and leads us to salvation."

STEP 4

"As our spirit evolves on our path to transformation, our resistant egos will persist; we hesitate at every juncture. The ego loves procrastination and stagnation – therefore, we must terminate our egos as our teachers, open our eyes and ears and hold our heads high during this period of personal growth. Our higher selves will comprehend the importance of this process. We will forever look at our brothers and sisters in a new light. Only those who are courageous enough to extensively explore their souls will find true peace."

Step 5

"Openly admitting the exact nature of our wrongs to another person is a daunting task. Our ego tries to keep us in darkness through separation, shame and fear, and it uses procrastination as an instrument to prevent personal growth. The ego never wants us to look inward, because if we look deeply enough, we may find our higher selves, which would in turn render the ego powerless.

With thorough self-assessment, we will become aware that we are as we see our fellow man. We recognize ourselves in each other and our true nature is based on love and truth. We require the two-way flow of energy that can only be found in fellowship.

Fear not; the liberating effect of vulnerability and total honesty carries benefits far beyond a simple feeling of relief – it provides us with a spiritual bond to our Creator and our fellow man. Therein lies sanity."

Step 6

"I tried to exchange my inheritance from God for the world I see. I focused on pain, illness, loss, age and death. Yet, with eternity we are promised perfect security and complete fulfillment.

When we are ready to remove our human defects of character and become willing to accept our true inheritance, we will be free of the illusions of fear and ego. This allows us to smoothly transform through time into eternity. the release of fear and the separation from the ego."

Step 7

"There appears to be a delicate balance between doing what is right and doing what we think needs to be done for survival in this chaotic world. yet, there is no need to distribute our efforts between love and fear – all undertakings need only to be directed toward the awareness of God's love and knowledge of His will for us.

We spend our lives achieving, struggling and resisting, and still the vessel we live in dies. Life's experiences deliver the wisdom to recognize that our human ambitions are of little worth. By no longer fearing death as we feared life, we are given a glimpse of heaven and an invitation to later cross the threshold into eternity.

With the time I have left here, I will remind myself every day that my true purpose is to learn, love, forgive, heal and teach. I will not project the darkness of my ego, but instead humbly convey the glowing light of God's love."

Step 8 & 9

"We are now aware that God's love and promise of eternity is more real than the illusion of life itself. We intuitively know that our journeys will reunite us with God, not as servants but as part of Him.
The sun has risen. Our wall of shadows can no longer compete with the brightness of God's light. Nevertheless, our transformation has delivered us to a road that narrows, and the insanity of ego will frequently revisit our human minds. Narrow roads are more difficult to navigate, so the ego will produce conflict and scream, "Go back, go back! This path is too difficult."

We must protect the brightness of the light and shelter our spirits with all our hearts. Be brave as we list those we have harmed and become willing to make amends with them all. We hold our heads high as we complete the next two steps on our paths to total transformation. The Twelve Promises are just around the corner as well as the new life that many before us have discovered through the steps.

Lastly, we must always remember that every situation, perceived correctly, is an opportunity to heal. Forgiveness is always an opportunity for peace, love and serenity."

*****

A Guided Meditation to start steps eight and nine:
"Close your eyes and sit quietly in a chair. Picture a closed mahogany door above your head. Now physically lift a hand above your head and slightly crack open the door. Visualize a narrow beam of light shining through the passageway you created. Now feel the misty burst of fresh air on your face and notice the aroma of lilacs lingering around you. Multiply the warmth of this experience by a trillion and you have not matched even a glimpse of eternity."

STEP 10

"I can change my mood by lucidly experiencing five minutes alone with the mind of God. My will controls my body and God's Will is my Spirit. I don't have a soul, I am a soul, I have a body. My soul has always been and always will be part of my Creator. By aligning with God's Will, I cannot escape or avoid truth. As a human I am unable to understand the mind of God, however, God's Will is easily to grasped. Prayer, mediation and quiet time will quickly align me with the reality and truth of God's Will."

*****

"Sit up straight, close your eyes and breathe only through your nose. Relax your jaw. With every exhale release the tension and toxins that separate you from perfection. After a minute, visualize your mind separating from your body, forming a white mist floating above you. For these brief minutes, allow only one thought: My mind holds only what I think with God.[20] Let each word shine with the meaning that God has given it.

*****

"As we continue with the steps, the worldly road gets narrower. Our behavioral options in life become fewer and fewer. Nevertheless, the reward of spiritual transformation becomes glaringly obvious: there is no better way to experience life than by having a clear mind that allows for God-Consciousness. Our goal is to "live in time as we will live in eternity: in the holy instant of the present moment.""

Step 11

"I used to wonder, if God exists and is so powerful and omnipotent, why would He allow man to go so far astray? If God is perfect love, then why do we have to suffer in this life? Why would God allow the forces of nature to kill, injure and destroy our homes and lives? Why wars, hunger, murder, rape, disease and injustice? Why would a just God give so much to a few, and so little to the masses? I had so many why's that I started to doubt the existence of God.

Once I stopped asking why, and made the decision to turn my life over to the care of God, the angst that had once controlled my chaotic life dissipated, and slowly the Spirit transformed my soul."

*****

"In this world, we have the option to make choices. One option is making the decision to accept that our ego-driven desires are the opposite of God's will. Everlasting peace is ours only when our wills are identical to God's will."

*****

"Comprehend the reality of God as perfect love and truth. God created man to share in eternity with Him, not as servants, but as part of Him. For man to rejoin with Him in eternity, we must be as He is. To be part of God in eternity, we must make the perpetual choice to pursue perfect love and truth. God granted us free will to make choices here on earth. As we strive to internalize perfect love and truth, we recognize that more will always be revealed. In this life, we transition from mere humans to the spiritual beings God desires us to be."

*****

"Many religions also profess that God has a plan for us. That is true in the enormous realm of eternity, but God having an exact plan for us in the same world in which we have unaltered free will is a conflicting concept. God grants us infinite possibilities to align with His ultimate plan, but as humans we have free agency to snub God at every turn, and many do. Some would preach that this would anger God and therefore those who snubbed God will be punished. I proclaim we leave it up to God. We are not here to judge. Not only should we not judge, we cannot judge; it's not in our job description."

*****

"Some fundamentalist religions use fear, guilt and shame to intimidate their flocks into adhering to a specific set of principles. These fear-based, maladapted teachings do not sit well with recovering people and may have contributed to the addiction process in the first place.

Regardless of past experiences, the recovering person usually finds a closer connection to God in recovery. Acceptance that everything is exactly as it should be, as well as living with awareness of the present, heals past wounds and past misconceptions over time."

*****

"The jubilation we feel by having a spiritual awakening is void of fear and doubt because we experience it in the moment. The only true thought that one can hold about the past is that it is not here."

STEP 12

"My sobriety alone brought me nothing. Like a prisoner released from a dungeon, beaten and emaciated, my newfound freedom from alcohol and cocaine did not bring me instant joy. My freedom delivered the question we all must eventually ask ourselves: Who am I?

As I started to learn not what I am but who I am, I recognized that the road to absolute peace continually gets narrower and narrower. When the road was no wider than the blade of a razor's edge, I became aware that I have one omnipotent purpose: total acceptance of God's will.

Accomplishments or labels do not define who I am, nor do organizations, employers or fellowships. The world I see is a percipience of me. How I see myself is how I see the world. My ego wants me to perceive a sickly universal illusion. When it succeeds, I comprehend the world as a fearful, merciless place. When I choose to see the world through happy eyes, I no longer judge my brothers and sisters. I recognize their innocence and simply accept them as they are – just like me.

At the moment of my spiritual awakening, I thought, Finally, God is smiling down at me. Now I know He never stopped smiling; I was simply missing in action. I have become aware that God is not positioned above me; rather, I am part of his creation and therefore I am part of Him.

"It's important to note that my step work did not finish with the completion of the twelve steps; it had just begun and it will never be complete. To keep the positive energy of recovery, we must also give it away. If we do not share our gift of recovery it will dissipate within a relatively short time. The shelf life of our healthy condition depends entirely on us actively carrying the message to those who still suffer.

On the day I got home from jail after my arrest, my chief pilot Captain

Gary Meermans called me at my home that had been ransacked by the police. He told me that when I get well I could keep what had happened to me a secret and in a few short years no one would remember that it was me who was arrested for possession of cocaine. Then he said, "On the other hand, if you share this experience, it just might help someone else recognize that they also need help." In that instant I decided to share my experience with others. Little did I know, that quick and undemanding decision would be the cornerstone of my long-term recovery. Sharing my story was the elementary stage in my life as a healer.

A day does not go by that I don't reach out to another recovering person. This is not a noble act; it's simply what I believe I need to do to maintain the incredible life that I have today.

There are so many people suffering from addiction that initially I was baffled about with whom I should spend my time. The solution presented itself: Do not seek out people who need help; help people who seek it."

*****

"Today I will make no decisions by myself..."

References

1. Tobin, Daniel R. *Transformational Learning: Renewing Your Company Through Knowledge and Skills.* Hoboken, New Jersey: John Wiley & Sons, Inc., 1996.
2. Anonymous. *Alcoholics Anonymous: The Big Book, 4th Ed.* New York City: Alcoholics Anonymous World Services, Inc., 2002.
3. Anonymous. *Alcoholics Anonymous: The Big Book, 4th Ed.* New York City: Alcoholics Anonymous World Services, Inc., 2002.
4. Anonymous. *Twelve Steps and Twelve Traditions, 48th printing.* New York City: Alcoholics Anonymous World Services, Inc., 2009.
5. Anonymous. *Alcoholics Anonymous: The Big Book, 4th Ed.* New York City: Alcoholics Anonymous World Services, Inc., 2002.
6. Schucman, Helen. *A Course in Miracles, Original Ed.* Omaha, Nebraska: Course in Miracles Society, 2009.
7. Schucman, Helen. *A Course in Miracles, Original Ed.* Omaha, Nebraska: Course in Miracles Society, 2009.
8. Anonymous. *Alcoholics Anonymous: The Big Book, 4th Ed.* New York City: Alcoholics Anonymous World Services, Inc., 2002.
9. Kaighan, Herb. *Twelve Steps to Spiritual Awakenings: Enlightenment for Everyone.* Torrance, CA: Capizon Publishing, 2010.
10. Schucman, Helen. *A Course in Miracles, Original Ed.* Omaha, Nebraska: Course in Miracles Society, 2009.
11. Kaighan, Herb. *Twelve Steps to Spiritual Awakenings: Enlightenment for Everyone.* Torrance, CA: Capizon Publishing, 2010.

12. Schucman, Helen. *A Course in Miracles, Original Ed.* Omaha, Nebraska: Course in Miracles Society, 2009.
13. Schucman, Helen. *A Course in Miracles, Original Ed.* Omaha, Nebraska: Course in Miracles Society, 2009.
14. Anonymous. *Alcoholics Anonymous: The Big Book, 4th Ed.* New York City: Alcoholics Anonymous World Services, Inc., 2002.
15. Anonymous. *Twelve Steps and Twelve Traditions, 48th printing.* New York City: Alcoholics Anonymous World Services, Inc., 2009.
16. Tolle, Eckhart. *A New Earth: Awakening to Your Life's Purpose.* New York City: Penguin Group, Inc., 2008.
17. Anonymous. *Twelve Steps and Twelve Traditions, 48th printing.* New York City: Alcoholics Anonymous World Services, Inc., 2009.
18. Schucman, Helen. *A Course in Miracles, Original Ed.* Omaha, Nebraska: Course in Miracles Society, 2009.
19. Anonymous. *Alcoholics Anonymous: The Big Book, 4th Ed.* New York City: Alcoholics Anonymous World Services, Inc., 2002.
20. Schucman, Helen. *A Course in Miracles, Original Ed.* Omaha, Nebraska: Course in Miracles Society, 2009.
21. Anonymous. *Twelve Steps and Twelve Traditions, 48th printing.* New York City: Alcoholics Anonymous World Services, Inc., 2009.
22. Kaighan, Herb. *Twelve Steps to Spiritual Awakenings: Enlightenment for Everyone.* Torrance, CA: Capizon Publishing, 2010.
23. Schucman, Helen. *A Course in Miracles, Original Ed.* Omaha, Nebraska: Course in Miracles Society, 2009.